Walt Disney's
TREASURY OF
Cartoon Classics

WALT DISNEY'S TREASURY OF Cartoon

Edited by Darlene Geis

HARRY N. ABRAMS, INC.,
PUBLISHERS, NEW YORK

Classics

Designer: Dirk Luykx

Library of Congress Catalog Card Number: 80-28072
ISBN 0-8109-0813-1

Originally published as *Walt Disney's Treasury of Stories
from Silly Symphonies*

Song Credits: "Who's Afraid of the Big Bad Wolf?" by Frank E.
Churchill, additional lyrics by Ann Ronell, © 1933 by Bourne
Co., copyright renewed. Used by permission. "The World Owes
Me a Living" lyrics by Larry Morey, music by Leigh Harline,
© 1934 by Bourne Co., copyright renewed. Used by permission.

This book is a co-production of Harry N. Abrams, Inc., and
Arnoldo Mondadori Editore S.p.A.

Printed and bound in Japan

Contents

Tales

Fables

Animal Stories

Nature Stories

Poems and Rhymes

The Silly Symphonies— How They Came to Be

Sound came to motion pictures with a bang when *The Jazz Singer* was released in 1927. Overnight, movies that did not talk, sing, and come equipped with sound effects appropriate to the action were outmoded.

The Disney studio had just embarked upon the first of its Mickey Mouse cartoons, and twenty-six-year-old Walt Disney, recognizing the future importance of the new technology, promptly decided to match the visual action on his drawing boards with recorded sound. A musical background and sound effects provided the most felicitous accompaniments to animation, but since movies were now called "talkies," it was clear that the cartoon characters would have to be given voices and lines to speak.

By 1929, the Mickey Mouse cartoons—with increasingly complex soundtracks and Walt's voice dubbed in for the Mouse's earnest falsetto—were a solid success. Carl Stalling, a musician with theater experience, was in charge of the orchestral background, which, more and more, was becoming the foremost element of the soundtrack. And that in turn led to Disney's next momentous decision. The Studio would

9

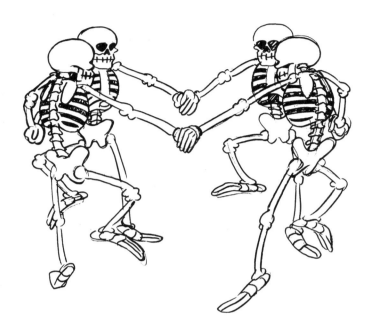

make a series of animated films that was not based upon its star, Mickey Mouse, at all, but instead would feature musical compositions mated to the animation, creating a mood rather than telling a story. They would call these new films Silly Symphonies.

The first of these revolutionary shorts was *The Skeleton Dance*, performed to an amusingly spooky score by Stalling which was borrowed in part from Grieg's "March of the Dwarfs." In it, a midnight graveyard, the sinister yowling of cats, and a clattering dance of four skeletons who had clambered out of their graves, cavorted until dawn, and then rattled back into their coffins set the mood—macabre yet entertaining—of this black-and-white cartoon brilliantly animated by Ub Iwerks, the Studio's top artist.

The movie exhibitors were somewhat tentative about this first Silly Symphony, but the public's immediate enthusiasm for *The Skeleton Dance* resulted in a long run in New York;

after that, the series found warm acceptance. Still, as extra insurance, the billing read, "Mickey Mouse Presents a Walt Disney Silly Symphony," although the Mouse, by 1930 an international celebrity, never appeared in any of them.

In the four years from 1929 to 1932, the Disney studio turned out twenty-eight Silly Symphonies. The earliest of these were mood pieces set to music and bearing titles such as *Springtime, Summer, Autumn, Night, Winter*. But soon Disney and his animators felt the need for characters and a story line to challenge their ingenuity further. *Mother Goose Melodies, The Ugly Duckling*, and *The Spider and the Fly* moved in that direction. The innovation of the Disney story board, on which the action of an entire short could be laid out scene by scene, fit in nicely with this new trend.

Then in 1932 another advance in motion picture technology created a new challenge. Technicolor had at last perfected an accurate color system for film, and Walt Disney lost no time in seeking the pot of gold at the end of that rainbow. He scrapped the black-and-white footage of his work in progress, *Flowers and Trees*, and remade it entirely in glorious Technicolor. The first Silly Symphony in color premiered with Irving Thalberg's *Strange Interlude* at Grauman's Chinese Theater in Hollywood and won an Academy Award for 1932.

From that time on all Silly Symphonies—forty-seven more of them—were in full color, though the Mickey Mouse cartoons continued to be produced in black and white until 1935. The brilliant palette inspired the Disney artists to new flights of fantasy and invention, often based on famous tales, fables, nursery rhymes, and poems.

In 1933, during the depths of the Depression, three little pigs danced and laughed their way into America's heart, thumbing their noses at adversity in the guise of a big bad wolf. As thousands cheered the picture, it cheered hundreds of thousands of economically beleaguered Americans who joined in the sentiments of Frank Churchill's hit song, "Who's Afraid of the Big Bad Wolf?" *The Three Little Pigs* was the most popular cartoon short ever, playing week in, week out in theaters across the land, often being billed above the feature film. Prestigious as well as popular, it won the Academy Award for best animated cartoon in the 1932–33 season.

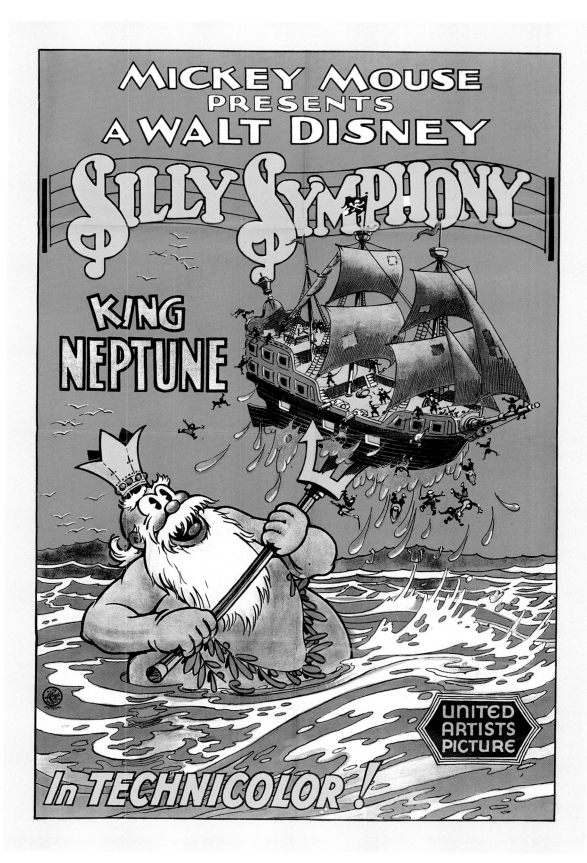

Six more golden Oscars came to Walt Disney's Silly Symphonies: *The Tortoise and the Hare* and *Three Orphan Kittens* for 1935, *The Country Cousin* for 1936, *The Old Mill* for 1937, *Ferdinand the Bull*, a special release, for 1938, and the last of the Silly Symphonies, a remake in color of *The Ugly Duckling*, for 1939.

By and large, the Mickey Mouse cartoons were far more popular all over the world—Topolino in Italy and Miki Kuchi in Japan were household names. But the Silly Symphonies had an importance for Disney that transcended box office popularity. They offered the Studio and its artists a chance to spread their wings, to dare new techniques and approaches, to create little jewels like *Wynken, Blynken, and Nod*— extravaganzas, but on a small scale. Here was the perfect laboratory and seedbed for the animator's art. Here new techniques were developed, experiments were dared, and the animated film came of age. Without Silly Symphonies, it is doubtful that Walt Disney's later feature-length masterpieces could have been realized.

Tales

The Three

Little Pigs

Once upon a time there were three little pigs whose mother sent them out into the world to seek their fortune. They each decided to build a house.

The first pig built his house of straw because that was the quickest and easiest way. No sooner was it finished when the merry little pig played a tune on his flute and danced a little jig. Then he sang:

> I built my house of straw.
> I built my house of hay.
> I toot my flute—
> I don't give a hoot—
> And play around all day.

After a while he skipped off down the path to see what his brothers were doing.

20

The second pig was hammering some sticks together to make his house. It didn't take long, and when it was finished, he picked up his fiddle and joined his brother in a jolly tune and a dance. While they played and danced, the second little pig sang:

I built my house of sticks.
I built my house of twigs.
With a hey-diddle-diddle
I play on my fiddle,
And dance all kinds of jigs.

Then both little pigs skipped off down the path to see what their brother was doing.

The third little pig was a practical pig. He was hard at work laying the bricks for his house. He wanted a solid, strong little house, a wolf-proof house, because he'd heard there

was a big bad wolf in the forest who liked to eat plump little pigs.

"Come on down and play," his brothers called to him. But Practical Pig went right on laying bricks while he recited:

> I build my house of stones.
> I build my house of bricks.
> I have no chance
> To sing and dance,
> For work and play don't mix.

"Ha, ha, ha," laughed the two little pigs. "Ho, ho, ho, ha, ha, ha, ha!" they laughed as they played and danced and sang. Practical Pig went on working while he warned

them, "I'll be safe and you'll be sorry when the big bad wolf comes around."

But the two little pigs laughed and laughed, and as they danced away toward the forest, they sang:

Who's afraid of the big bad wolf?
Big bad wolf, big bad wolf?
Who's afraid of the big bad wolf?
Tra la la la la!

Meanwhile, from behind a tree, the wolf was watching, and his mouth watered at the sight of the two plump pigs. He moved closer and closer, hiding behind one tree after another until—he was close enough to pounce!

The two little pigs suddenly saw the big bad wolf with his mouth wide open ready to grab them, and they turned and ran for home.

The first pig ran into his straw house, pulling the "Welcome" mat in at the last moment. Then he slammed the door in the wolf's face. The wolf knocked at the door, coaxing, "Little pig, little pig, let me in."

"Not by the hair on my chinny-chin-chin. I won't let you in!" replied the pig.

"Then I'll huff and I'll puff and I'll blow your house in!" snarled the wolf.

And he huffed and he puffed and he blew the straw house down. He grabbed at the little pig, but the pig ran as fast as his legs could carry him to his brother's house of sticks. He got there just in time and slammed the door in the wolf's face.

"Curses," growled the wolf as he rattled the locked door.

The two little pigs were shaking with fright, and they hid under the rug.

But the wolf had an idea. "I'll fool them," he said to himself. Then he called out loud, "Those pigs are too smart for me. I'm going home." The wolf hid behind some bushes while he made the sounds of running footsteps fading away in the distance.

The two little pigs waited awhile, and when they heard nothing more from the wolf, they looked at one another and said, "He's gone!" They crawled out from under the rug and began to dance happily around the room, singing:

Who's afraid of the big bad wolf?
Big bad wolf, big bad wolf?
Who's afraid of the big bad wolf?
Tra la la la la!

Suddenly there was a knock on the door. It was the wolf, hiding under a sheepskin and looking like a little lamb.

"Who's there?" asked the pigs in trembly voices.

"I'm a poor little sheep with no place to sleep. Can you open the door and let me in?" asked the wolf in a high squeaky voice. But the pigs looked out the window and saw the big mouth and teeth under the white fleece.

"Not by the hair on our chinny-chin-chins. You can't fool us with that old sheepskin!" they called.

"Then I'll huff and I'll puff and I'll blow your house in!" snarled the angry wolf.

And he huffed and he puffed and he blew the house down.

Off raced the two little pigs to their brother's house. They dashed into the brick house and dived under the bed while Practical Pig calmly fastened the chain on the door.

"I told you to be careful of the wolf," he scolded, "but we're snug and safe here." Practical Pig sat down at his piano and began to play and sing:

Who's afraid of the big bad wolf?
Big bad wolf, big bad wolf?
Who's afraid of the big bad wolf?
Tra la la la la!

Soon the two little pigs crawled out from under the bed and danced and sang along.

Meanwhile the big bad wolf disguised himself as a peddler selling brushes, and he knocked on the door.

"Who's there?" asked Practical Pig.

"I'm selling nice brushes," answered the wolf.

The little pig opened the door on the chain, reached through the crack, and grabbed one of the wolf's brushes. Then he poked and whacked at the wolf with it while the wolf howled in pain.

"That'll teach him," said Practical Pig as he closed the door.

The angry wolf shouted, "I'll huff and I'll puff and I'll blow your house in!"

So he huffed and he puffed until he grew red in the face, but nothing happened. The three little pigs were safe inside, laughing and dancing and singing.

The wolf huffed and puffed some more until he grew blue in the face, but he couldn't budge the house of bricks. Finally he leaped up on the roof and climbed into the chimney.

When Practical Pig heard the footsteps on his roof and saw soot dropping down his chimney, he knew just what to do. He got a can of turpentine and poured it into the big pot of hot water that was boiling in the fireplace.

When the wolf came sliding down the chimney, he dropped PLOP! in the hot turpentine. He let out one great howl and shot straight up the chimney. When he landed on the ground he ran, and kept running, until he disappeared into the distance, never to be seen again.

Inside, two happy little pigs were singing and dancing while Practical Pig played the tune on the piano:

> *Who's afraid of the big bad wolf?*
> *Big bad wolf, big bad wolf?*
> *Who's afraid—*

Mischievously, Practical Pig banged on the wooden piano KNOCK, KNOCK, KNOCK! Two little pigs, thinking it was the wolf at the door again, dove under the bed, while Practical Pig laughed and laughed. He had the last laugh after all.

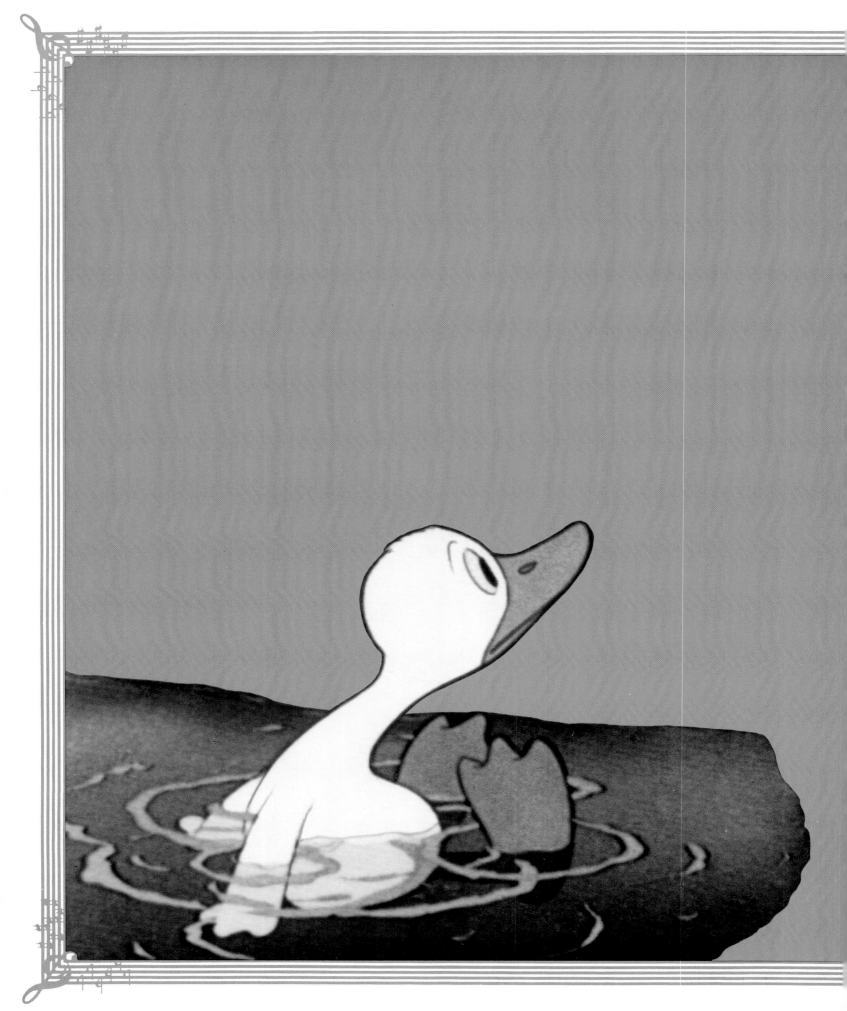

The Ugly Duckling

In the summer, when the hay was stacked in the meadows and the reeds and dock leaves grew as thick as a forest at the water's edge, a mother duck was sitting on her nest in the tall grass. There were five eggs keeping warm beneath her, and she sat quietly, waiting for them to hatch.

Mother Duck was quite tired of sitting, for it was taking a long time. At last, one by one, the eggs began to move and then to crack. "Cheep, cheep, cheep, cheep!" said four of the tiny ducklings as they poked their heads out of the shells. Then they stumbled out and fluffed their yellow down. They looked like soft little butterballs with bright button eyes, and their mother beamed at her little beauties proudly.

But what was this? The biggest egg still lay in the nest, unhatched. Wearily, Mother Duck settled herself on top of it. "How much longer is this going to take?" she wondered.

Just then Father Duck came by to see how she was getting along.

"This one big egg is very slow," Mother Duck explained, "but do look at the four that have already hatched. They are the most beautiful ducklings I have ever seen. They look exactly like you, my dear."

It was true, thought Father Duck preening his feathers. The ducklings did him proud.

A day or so later, the large gray egg finally moved, the shell cracked, and finally a clumsy youngster tumbled out. "Honk," he said in a most unduck-like voice. Father Duck and Mother Duck looked with astonishment at this strange baby and then at each other.

"That is a monstrous big duckling," said Father Duck.

"None of the others look like that. Could you have been sitting on a turkey egg by mistake, my dear?"

Mother Duck was puzzled herself as she examined the awkward creature. Even its color was wrong. It was gray instead of yellow.

"Well," she said. "We'll soon find out if he's a turkey chick or a duckling. Into the water with him, whether he likes it or not. He can sink or swim."

And she called her little brood to follow her down to the pond. The day was fine, and the clumsy gray duckling walked happily behind his smaller brothers and sisters, eager to join in their play. But they tripped him and nipped at him with their beaks until, by the time they reached the pond, he was almost in tears.

The four little ducklings waddled into the water right away, but the Ugly Duckling stood unhappily on the bank, afraid of what further mischief the others might do to him.

"Into the water with you," his mother scolded. "Don't just stand there like a great ugly booby!"—and she shoved him into the pond. Much to everyone's surprise, the Ugly Duckling swam. Not only that, he swam strongly and well.

When it was time to go home, the mother duck called her ducklings to follow her out of the pond. The Ugly Duckling was last in line again, and the others turned on him just as he was clambering up the bank and knocked him back into the water.

"Go away!" they shouted. "Don't tag after us, you ugly thing!" And off they waddled after their mother, who had never a backward glance for the Ugly Duckling.

The poor little fellow sat in the pond, his tears falling splash, splash, splash into the still water. "Why don't they want to play with me?" he wondered. "Why does everyone— even my mother—call me ugly?"

At that he looked down into the water, all rippled now from his splashing tears. The reflection on the rippled surface was indeed bumpy and strange—yes, really funny looking. "No

wonder they call me ugly," thought the duckling. "I will run away deep into the forest and hide so no one can see how ugly I am."

It was dark and frightening in the forest, and the little duckling felt very lonely. He was glad when he heard a cheeping sound overhead. Looking up he saw a nest of young birds on a low branch, and the duckling called to them, "Can I play with you?"

"Sure, come and join us," peeped the birds.

Soon the Ugly Duckling was settled happily in the nest amidst his new little friends. They were all having a fine time together when suddenly there was a beating of wings just above them and a shrill, scolding bird cry. The mother and father bird had returned to the nest and were very angry to find a big stranger in with their youngsters.

"Out! Out!" they shrilled. "Go find your own family and leave our nest to us!"

The Ugly Duckling clambered out of the nest as fast as he could and scurried off to the rushes at the edge of the pond. "It is because I am so ugly that nobody wants me," he thought sadly. "I will just have to stay all by myself."

He swam about on the pond alone for many weeks, managing to find lily roots and other things to eat so he wouldn't starve. But oh, he was so lonely with no one to talk to, no one to play with, no one who loved him or whom he could love. At least, though, there was no one to tease him or call him ugly or treat him cruelly. The Ugly Duckling sighed as he paddled about all by himself.

Then one day a group of little birds swam by, and they looked at the ugly duckling and asked him if he'd like to play. The duckling could scarcely believe his good luck. They all played together the whole afternoon, and not once did anyone nip him or chase him or call him ugly.

Near the end of the day his new friends said, "Why don't you come home with us?"

The Ugly Duckling swam across the pond with them, and there he saw the most glorious bird he had ever set eyes on. Brilliantly white with a long, graceful neck, this creature sailed with queenlike majesty to meet them. The duckling was so stunned by her beauty that he forgot to hide, forgot to turn away to conceal his ugliness.

The great white bird glided closer to him and lifted her wing. Too late the duckling realized that now he would be beaten and driven off as he deserved. But instead the wing encircled him gently—he had never felt anything as soft as the down on its underside.

"You are a new one!" said the bird. "Where have you been, my little lost swan?"

"He is the most beautiful of us all!" exclaimed the other little swans.

The Ugly Duckling looked down into the calm water of the pond and saw his own reflection. Lo and behold! Although it was not yet a great swan, the little swan looking up at him was far from ugly.

"Come, my darlings," said the mother swan. "Let us go home," and proudly the family of swans sailed out on the pond.

Watching them float by, the mother duck said to her family, "There go the swans. Aren't they the most beautiful creatures you have ever seen?"

And the birds, flying back to their nest, saw the stately swans and said, "It must be wonderful to be so graceful and handsome."

Holding his head high, the little swan followed his new family, happy to know where he belonged.

The

Pied Piper

In the pretty little walled German town of Hamelin, almost five hundred years ago, the people were having a terrible time. The trouble was—RATS!

Rats fought the dogs and killed the cats. Rats bit babies in their cradles. Rats ate everything in sight—cheese, sausages, fruit. And the noise of their squeaking in fifty different sharps and flats drowned out everyone's conversation.

At last the people grew tired of this plague of rats, and they demanded that the mayor do something about it. The mayor spoke to the crowd of angry citizens gathered near the city gate.

"As mayor of this fair city," he said, "I promise to give this bag of gold to anyone who can rid us of these terrible rats. I would sell my ermine gown for a trap, a trap that would

46

really work on these monstrous rats. I would..." But just then a voice rang out from the back of the crowd.

"Stop!"

The crowd turned to look; the mayor turned to look; even the rats turned to look. There stood the strangest figure. He was dressed from head to foot in a queer long coat, half-yellow, half-red. He was tall and thin with sharp blue eyes, long straight

hair, and an odd smile that played about his mouth. And he
carried a long, slender pipe tied to the end of a red-and-yellow-
striped scarf that hung about his neck.

"I'll rid your town of rats," he called out.

"All right," the mayor said. "You'll get the bag of gold—
if indeed you know how to get rid of these pesky rats."

"Please, Your Honor," said the man, "I'm able, by means
of a secret charm, to draw all creatures living beneath the
sun—whether they creep or swim or fly or run—after me. I
mostly use my charm on creatures that harm people: the mole,
the bat, the snake, the rat." He smiled a little smile as if
he knew what magic he commanded. "People call me the Pied
Piper."

Then the Piper started to blow on his pipe while his skinny
fingers moved over the stops. Before three shrill notes had
sounded there was a muttering that grew to a grumbling that
grew to a mighty rumbling, and out of the houses tumbled
hundreds of rats. Big rats, little rats, thin rats, brawny rats,
brown, gray, black, and tawny rats; old ones, young ones,
father rats, mother rats, sisters, brothers, uncles, cousins,

whole families of rats followed the Piper as if their lives depended upon it.

From street to street he went, piping his tune while thousands of rats poured out of the houses and followed behind him, dancing. The Piper led the army of rats through the city gate and down the road beyond the town.

When the last rat passed through the gate, a great cheer went up from the people watching on the walls. They

slammed the gate closed and looked at their ratless town with joy and relief.

The Piper, meanwhile, pointed down the road to the rats. There in the distance was a gigantic Swiss cheese, a towering cheese gleaming like some magical rat fairyland.

The rats needed no urging. Off they raced, past the Piper, falling all over one another in their haste to reach the cheese. One by one they disappeared through the holes into the cheese until every last one of them was out of sight.

Then the Piper started back to town. The mayor and townspeople were waiting on top of the wall. The gate was closed.

"I'll take my bag of gold now!" the Piper called up to the mayor.

"What!" exclaimed the mayor. "All you did was pipe a tune!" And the people chorused, "Yes. All you did was pipe a tune."

"Here's your pay." And the mayor tossed one piece of gold down to the Piper. The Piper caught it and glared up at the people. "Don't trifle with me," he warned. "Folks who make me angry may find that I pipe another tune. I'll pipe your children right out of the town."

"Blow your pipe until you burst," the mayor retorted.

"Yes, blow your pipe until you burst!" the townspeople repeated.

Once more the Piper put his long pipe to his lips. And before he blew three notes, three sweet soft notes, there was a rustling and a bustling of merry crowds hustling; small feet were pattering, and little hands were clapping; children were chattering, and out ran all the boys and girls. They dropped whatever they were doing, and with sparkling eyes they danced and skipped toward the sound of the piping.

The city gate burst open and out danced the children, shouting and laughing as they followed the Piper and his tune down the road. One little lame boy on crutches hobbled after the others, the last of the children to pass through the gate.

The mayor and the people watched the children leave, struck dumb with horror. But when they saw Koppelberg Hill in the distance, they were relieved. "He never can cross that

mighty mountain," the people said. "He'll have to stop there, and the children will come back."

But no! As they reached the mountain's side, the Piper blew a call, and a marvelous thing happened. The side of the mountain opened wide, as if a wonderful cavern were hollowed out there. The Piper marched in with the children running after him. There were toys and candy waiting for them, and the sounds of their delighted laughter rang across the fields.

The little lame boy was almost left behind, but the Piper beckoned, and the boy dropped his crutches and ran. He ran right inside the mountain to join the others. The Piper threw his crutches out—the boy would never need them again. And the mountain closed on the laughter of the happy children playing forever inside.

Santa's Workshop

ar away up at the North Pole, where the aurora borealis spreads its colored lights across the nighttime sky, Santa's workshop is bustling with activity. It is December, and the elves who are Santa's helpers are working overtime to fill all the Christmas orders. The factory where toys are made is going full blast with smoke pouring from every chimney.

Bulging sacks of mail are delivered to Santa every day. Each letter has a request from a boy or girl somewhere in the world asking for his or her heart's desire. And jolly old Santa reads them all.

"Here's one from Molly," he says. "Hmm, she wants a talking, walking doll." Santa looks up Molly's name in a big book with the help of one of his elves.

"It's OK," says the elf. "Molly's been a pretty good girl all year."

So Santa puts a big "yes" after her name.

Next Santa picks up a very long letter. It's so long it almost reaches the floor. "Billy wants just about everything in the shop," Santa chuckles. "Trains, skates, an airplane, a ball, a bat. My, oh, my!"

But the elf has found Billy's name in the book, and he shakes his head. "Billy didn't wash his ears," he announces.

"Too bad," Santa says, and he writes "soap" after Billy's name.

Then Santa bustles off to see how things are faring in the workshop. Dozens of busy elves sit at long tables assembling the toys. Some saw pieces of wood and carve them into horses. Others fasten rockers onto the legs, glue manes of hair to the necks, and attach reins to the mouths. Then off the rocking horses go to the paint department for a coat of white or brown or dappled gray.

At one table the dollmakers mold beautiful faces. Artists paint the lips and cheeks and eyes, and wigmakers curl wavy blond hair, which is fitted to each doll's head. The head is

attached to a soft, stuffed body, and tailors sew pretty dresses of pink or green or yellow with ruffled skirts for the dolls to wear.

As each doll is finished, she is passed on to Santa for a final inspection and one last important detail. Santa picks up the doll and bends her toward him.

"Say 'mama,'" he orders.

"Ma-Ma!" says the doll, and Santa stamps his OK on her.

Rubber balls, sailboats, bicycles, and airplanes pass by Santa, who looks them over carefully. Those that he OKs move on down to the loading room. Those that need fixing are put up on a shelf. As Santa reaches up to put a broken airplane on the shelf, he accidentally knocks some mechanical toys to the floor.

Lo and behold! The toys begin to move. A little toy band strikes up a march, and the tin soldiers strut, hup-two-three-four, followed by a parade of toys. Stuffed animals, dolls, wagons, trucks move along on the floor behind the marching soldiers. Santa opens his enormous brown bag, and all the toys follow the tin soldier, hup-two-three-four, right into the bag.

And now the calendar says December 24, Christmas Eve. There is no time to lose, for Santa must start on his long journey delivering toys to all the boys and girls all over the world for Christmas morning.

The big old sleigh is brought out of the barn and given a new coat of paint by some of the elves. They polish the metal runners until they gleam.

The reindeer are taken out of their stalls—Donner and Blitzen, Dasher and Dancer, Prancer and Vixen, Comet and Cupid; all eight of them must be readied for the important night's work. Snowflakes are beginning to fall in the courtyard where the groom-elves are brushing the reindeer's coats, polishing their antlers, and shining their hooves. Everything must be just right for Santa on this night, a night that all have planned and worked so hard for throughout the year.

At last the sleigh is loaded with the jam-packed sack of toys. The reindeer are harnessed and eager to be off. Hundreds of little elves, their labor finished for another year, gather before the factory to see Santa off and wish him a good

journey. Up Santa climbs on his sleigh. He waves good-bye to his cheering workers, snaps his whip as a signal that it's time to be off, and away the reindeer go. Up, up into the frosty sky they soar, where the smiling moon and the Christmas star welcome the jolly old fellow who will bring joy to the children tomorrow.

Lullaby Land

"Rock-a-bye, baby," mother sang as she tucked the baby into bed. He snuggled down under his patchwork quilt, hugging his toy dog.

Rock-a-bye, baby,
on the treetop!
When the wind blows
the cradle will rock. . . .

The cradle swayed high up in the night sky, close to the stars and the smiling Man in the Moon.

When the bough breaks
the cradle will fall,
And down will come baby,
cradle and all.

Down, down, down through the night sky tumbled the

baby, his toy dog, and the cradle. And they landed with a soft thump on the patchwork hills of Lullaby Land.

What a magical place it was! There stood a bush with powder puffs hanging from it and cans of sweet-smelling talcum. The talcum snowed down on the baby while the puffs gently patted the powder all over him.

Meanwhile the toy dog discovered a wonderful rattle tree. He was sniffing around its trunk when suddenly the tree shook its branches hard and dozens of little rattles went clatter, click, rap, tap, and clap, startling the toy dog half out of his wits and frightening him away.

But what new sound was this? The baby and his dog heard music and the thump thump of marching, and they ran to watch the Lullaby Land parade go by. Cups, dishes, and

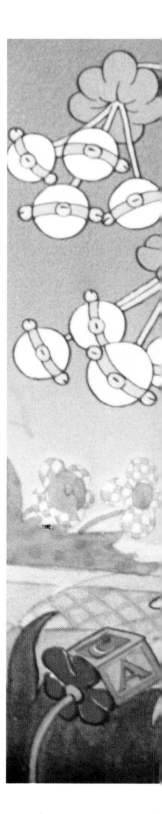

spoons led the way. Babies' bottles followed, with comb and brush, diaper pins, and diapers in a long procession—all the familiar things of a baby's day.

The baby laughed to see so many of his old friends, and he and his dog followed the parade, playing leapfrog along the way until suddenly they came to the entrance of the Forbidden Garden.

> BABY STAY AWAY
> KEEP OUT
> DON'T ENTER
> NO NO
> GO BACK

The signs at the gate were printed in big bold letters. But the baby couldn't read, nor could his toy dog. So in they

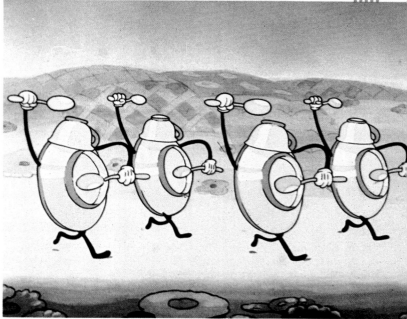

went through the gate where sharp knives and forks leaned dangerously against the wall.

The Forbidden Garden was filled with all the things that are bad for babies—pocketknives, scissors, hot curling irons, sharp tacks and pins, fountain pens, ink that makes terrible black spots—and, worst of all, things that could be used for dangerous mischief.

The baby found a beautiful watch tree growing next to a hammer bush. What an interesting combination! There were round gold pocket watches just like grandpa's hanging from the tree. The baby plucked a hammer from the bush and whacked at a watch. He whacked at another watch with the hammer. Smash, bang! In no time, all the watches were broken, and so was a cuckoo clock.

"Cuckoo! Cuckoo!" the bird scolded angrily as it popped out from the clock at the baby. Frightened, the baby scurried away.

What did he come to next but a big box of matches,

74

something he had never before been able to touch. Now was his chance! But just as the baby managed to climb up the side of the matchbox, his dog came along and tried to pull him away. The baby paid no attention, and up he climbed into the matches.

As he was waving one of the little sticks around, he was amazed to see it suddenly light up. He laughed at the funny trick until it felt HOT! The baby dropped the match quickly, but the mischief had been done. It fell onto a pile of loose matches—and whoosh! The matches flamed up into a bright orange fire.

The toy dog was barking for the baby to come down, and this time he paid attention. Down the baby climbed and away he and his dog scampered as fast as they could. For right behind them were two flaming matches trying to burn them.

Just in the nick of time the baby and dog came to a pool of water with a big bar of soap floating in it. One jump ahead of the burning matches, they leaped onto the soap bar and sailed for the opposite shore.

When the matches hit the water, their flames hissed out and turned into fat puffs of smoke. The puffs of smoke then turned into bogeymen. These creatures made such terrible

faces they frightened the poor baby and dog who took to their
heels and ran out of the Forbidden Garden.

While they were hiding behind a friendly baby-bottle tree,
catching their breath, a strange voice sang out, "Peek-a-
boo!" Again the baby and his dog were startled. But at that
moment a kindly old man with a long white beard and a large
sack filled with sand stepped out from behind a candy-cane
bush. He sang softly, and as he sang he sprinkled sand on the
flowers, and they went to sleep.

It was the Sandman, and when he sprinkled a shower of sand on the baby and his dog, they rubbed their eyes . . . and closed them . . . and fell fast asleep at last.

And there they were, sleeping safe and sound at home again, in the baby's own cradle, all the rest of the night.

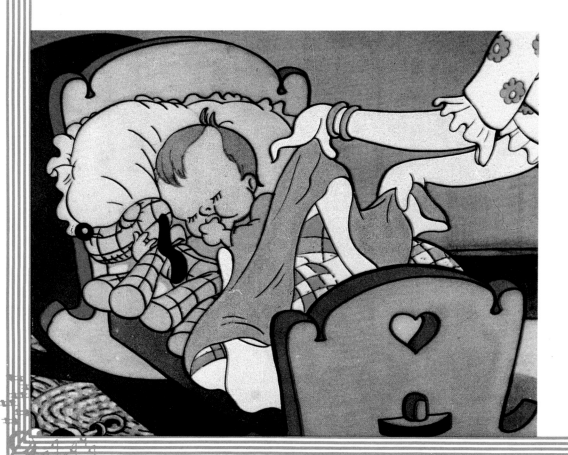

Fables

The Grasshopper and the

Ants

Once there was a carefree grasshopper, who fiddled and sang and danced all the summer long. As he jumped and hopped through the tall green grass he sawed away at his fiddle and sang:

> *Oh the world owes me a living,*
> *Tra la-la la-la la-la la-la.*
> *The good book says*
> *"The world provides."*
> *There's food on every tree.*
> *Why should anyone have to work?*
> *Not me!*
> *Oh the world owes me a living,*
> *Tra la-la la-la la-la la-la.*

The grasshopper nearly hopped right on top of some ants who were hard at work hauling a kernel of corn up a hill. He looked at them pulling and straining, and he shook his head and asked:

Why are you working
All through the day?
A summer day
Is a time to play!

But the ants toiled on up the hill. "We can't play," they replied. "Winter will soon be here." And they continued hauling the corn, sawing carrots into chunks, and storing everything away against the winter months ahead.

The grasshopper paid no attention and went his way singing and dancing. When he felt hungry he reached for a juicy green leaf to nibble; when he felt thirsty he tipped a bluebell to his mouth and took a sip of nectar. And when he felt like spitting, he just let go a great big spurt of grasshopper juice. It nearly splashed on a young ant named Andy, who was pulling a cart of cherries to the storehouse.

Andy slipped and fell in a mud puddle, and the grasshopper laughed and then beckoned to the ant. "Come here, son," he called. He tucked his fiddle under his chin and sang:

The world owes me a living,
Tra la-la la-la la-la la-la.
You should soil your Sunday pants,
Like those other foolish ants,
Well, no—let's sing and play and dance!

The little ant was delighted. He dropped his heavy burden and joined the grasshopper. They were both dancing merrily, when all of a sudden a procession of ants carrying the Queen of Ants on her throne stopped alongside them. The Queen stepped down and walked toward Andy, frowning. The little ant took one look at her angry face, picked up his load, and ran off to store it away, while the grasshopper laughed at his fright.

But the Queen of Ants was not amused. "You'll change your tune when winter comes and the ground is white with

snow," she warned him. The grasshopper doffed his hat and bowed deeply. "Wintertime is a long way off, madam," he said. "Do you dance? Let's go!" And tapping his foot in time to his fiddling, he sang:

The other ants can work all day.
Why don't you try the grasshopper's way?
Come on, let's sing and dance and play!
Oh the world owes me a living,
Tra la-la la-la la-la la-la.

The Queen of Ants had no time for his foolishness, and she turned away angrily and hurried off to work with the other busy ants. The grasshopper shrugged and went on playing and singing.

The golden days of summer seemed endless. The grasshopper, without a care in the world, enjoyed every lazy minute. The ants toiled away from sunup to sundown, lugging food from here and there and storing it snugly in their house.

But the world was beginning to change. Leaves drifted down from the trees, first a few at a time, then more and more. At last, when stronger winds started to blow, brown and yellow and orange leaves whirled down. They were too dry to eat, and the grasshopper was getting very hungry. It grew colder, and the ants scurried into their house for the winter, shutting their door behind them.

One freezing gray day the wind blew millions of snowflakes everywhere. The ants' house was covered with snow.
The ground was hidden under a blanket of white. There were
only bare twigs on the trees. The poor starving grasshopper
shivered out in the cold with nowhere to go, nothing to eat,
and only his fiddle and bow to keep him company.

Then in the distance he saw something delicious! One last
leaf still clung to a twig. The grasshopper struggled through
the snow, his hands stretching toward that wonderful leaf.
"Food!" he cried. "Food!" But just as he reached the tree, a
gust of wind whisked the leaf away. The grasshopper was left
standing alone in the falling snow as he watched the last leaf
twisting and turning in the wind, moving farther and farther
away from him, until at last it was gone.

Now the wind blew harder, whistling sharply, and the
grasshopper grew colder and colder. He trembled with a chill
and finally turned blue with cold and dropped to the snowy

ground. He thought it was all over for him, but at that moment, he spied the doorway of the ants' house.

Somehow the grasshopper dragged himself to the door and knocked. Then he collapsed in the snow, too cold, too hungry to make another move. The ants, who had been enjoying a big banquet in their warm house, opened the door and saw the poor frozen grasshopper lying there. No longer was he the merry singer of the summer.

A dozen ants scurried out and hauled the grasshopper into their cozy house. They put his frozen feet into a tub of warm water. They wrapped him in blankets and fed him hot soup, and little by little the grasshopper's color returned, he stopped trembling, and he began to feel like himself.

But then he saw the Queen of Ants striding toward him, looking at him sternly. The grasshopper began to tremble again, this time with fright. Would the Queen throw him out in the cold to freeze and starve?

Piteously the grasshopper pleaded:

> Oh, Madam Queen,
> Wisest of ants,
> Please, please,
> Don't throw me out.
> Let me join you.
> Give me another chance.

The Queen handed the grasshopper his fiddle and said severely:

> Just those
> Who work may stay.

The poor grasshopper took his fiddle, got his hat, and prepared to go out into the cold once more. But the Queen continued:

So take your fiddle—
And PLAY!

Joyfully, the grasshopper put his hat down, raised his
fiddle to his chin, and started tapping his foot. Then he sang:

I owe the world a living,
Tra la-la la-la la-la la-la.
I've been a fool
The whole year long.
Now I'm singing
A different song.
You were right,
I was wrong.
Tra la-la la-la la-la la-la.

Now the ants who had worked so hard all summer took
their turn to enjoy themselves. They all began to dance to the

grasshopper's tune, and even the Queen of Ants joined in the fun while the grasshopper sang:

Now I'm singing
A different song.
I owe the world a living,
Tra la-la la-la la-la la-la.

The Tortoise

There once was a fast-talking, fast-moving hare who used to tease his friend the tortoise about his slowness. The tortoise tried not to be bothered by the hare's taunts, but one day in front of all the other animals it got to be just too much, and in a fit of annoyance the tortoise said, "Let's settle this once and for all. Let's run a race and see who wins. And if I do, no more of your jokes about how slow I am."

The hare laughed. "*That's* a joke," he said. "I can run rings around you, and you know it."

"Never mind," the tortoise answered. "Just stop boasting, and let's get going with the race."

So a day was set for the great event, and all the animals crowded into bleachers to watch. The hare strode up to the starting line waving and bowing to the crowd as though he

were already the winner. The tortoise modestly took his place after first trying to shake the hare's hand like a good sport.

The starter blew his whistle, the racers crouched on their mark, and at a blast from the starting gun, they were off. The hare was down the road like a smoking streak, his speed twirling the tortoise on his shell as if he were a spinning top. By the time the tortoise got himself in gear, the speedy hare was almost out of sight.

"Never mind," the tortoise told himself. "Straight and steady does it. Just keep going." And he did, though even some snails passed him on the road.

Meanwhile the hare was whizzing along. When he looked back, he couldn't even see the tortoise. "Well," he thought, "no use knocking myself out when I'm way ahead." And he stopped in the shade of a tree. "May as well refresh myself with a little nap." And in two seconds he was fast asleep.

But the tortoise kept plodding along, and pretty soon he

came to the tree where the hare was snoozing. On he went, looking neither to the right nor to the left. A few minutes later the hare woke up with a start and saw that the tortoise had passed him. "This'll be easy," he said to himself. And off he sped, waving tauntingly to the tortoise as he passed him.

Fast as he was moving, the hare saw from the corner of his eye a sign that said "Girls' School." He also managed to glimpse some of the girls, a row of adorable little bunnies sitting on a rock watching the race.

"This is too good to miss," he decided as he came to a screeching stop. Then he ambled over to talk to the bunnies.

"Oh, isn't he big and handsome?" one bunny squealed to the others, and they all nearly tumbled off the rock giggling.

"You're pretty cute yourselves," said the hare, sticking his chest out and strutting back and forth in front of them.

Just then the tortoise came stepping along, looking neither to the right nor to the left.

"Yoo-hoo," called the bunnies. "Want to stop here and talk to us for a while?"

"Got no time," the tortoise muttered, and on he went.

"I've got lots of time," the hare bragged, "and I'll still beat the old slowpoke." And he and the bunnies laughed and laughed at the poor tortoise.

"Let me show you a few speedy tricks," said the hare,

delighted to impress his pretty audience. The girls watched him with round eyes.

He picked up a bow and arrow, shot the arrow, placed an apple on his head, and ran twenty feet to where the arrow neatly split the apple in half.

"He sure can run like sixty," sighed one of the bunnies.

"Heck," said the hare. "I was only warming up."

But the bunnies were getting worried about the race.

"Don't you think you'd better go?" they asked.

"I've got lots of time," said the cocky hare. "Watch what I can do on the tennis court."

And he picked up a racquet and ball, sent a smashing serve over the net, leaped over the net and returned the serve, leaped back and volleyed, and kept that up until he was quite out of breath.

"Oooh," sighed the admiring bunnies. But the hare heard another sound in the distance, the sound of cheering, and it wasn't for him.

"Be seeing you, girls," he called over this shoulder. And off he streaked.

Up ahead he could see the finish line and the crowds waiting for the end of the race. There was the tortoise, almost at the line. The hare ran like he'd never run before, and he began to gain on the tortoise. But at the last minute the determined tortoise picked up his shell and his legs *moved!* Just as the hare nearly caught up with him, the tortoise s-t-r-e-t-c-h-e-d till his head touched the finish line.

"The tortoise wins—by a neck!" shouted the judge.

The crowd lifted the victorious tortoise on their shoulders, and they cheered and cheered, while the braggart hare, for once, had nothing to say.

Moral: Slow and steady wins the race.

The Country

Cousin

666

nce upon a time a country mouse was invited
to visit his cousin in the big city. Now Abner had
everything a mouse could desire in the country—a
snug little cottage with a pantry full of peas and barley, scraps
of cheese, and nuts; and outside his house were beautiful
woods and fields where he could roam freely.

But, thought Abner, maybe it would be nice to live in
splendor for a while with Cousin Monte. So off he went to the
big city for a taste of high life.

At the entrance to his cousin's large and impressive
house, Abner knocked loudly with his umbrella. Monte
opened the door a crack. "Sh-sh-sh," he whispered as he
pulled Abner inside. "It's not safe to make so much noise
around here. You're not in the wide open spaces."

Abner followed his cousin into the house. He was hungry
after his journey and was happy to see a large piece of cheese
conveniently awaiting him right on the floor. How thoughtful
of his cousin to set out a tasty snack.

But as Abner was about to reach for the cheese, Monte grabbed his arm. "Don't touch it!" he warned. "It's in a mousetrap." And he poked the cheese with Abner's umbrella. BAM! The trap snapped shut on the umbrella, and Abner shivered to think how it would have felt on *him!*

"Follow me for some real eats," his cousin ordered. And he led the country mouse into a great banquet room. On the long table was a feast the likes of which Abner had never imagined. Cheeses, breads, cakes, and all manner of dainties, strange jars and bottles, brightly colored gelatins, snowy mounds of whipped cream topped with dazzling red cherries—it was enough to make the country mouse's head reel.

"Go ahead, help yourself," whispered Monte, who was nibbling a bit of this and a bit of that, moving furtively and looking over his shoulder as though danger lurked behind every delicious treat.

Abner did not have to be asked twice. He gazed up at a mountain of Swiss cheese and broke off a generous chunk. He took a stalk of crisp celery and had just started to munch on it blissfully when Monte signaled him with his finger to his lips. "Not so much noise!" he whispered.

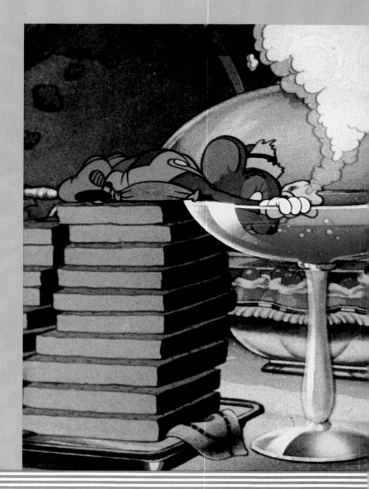

But Abner was racing from one side of the table to the other in an ecstasy of fine dining. He dipped his hand into a bowl of whipped cream and licked it greedily. Meanwhile, his city cousin was nibbling daintily, dabbing at his whiskers with a handkerchief after every delicate mouthful, and watching Abner with disapproval. Abner mopped his face with his red bandanna and then blew his nose loudly.

"Sh-sh-sh-sh!" whispered Monte.

On the other side of the table an open jar that said "Mustard" looked inviting. Abner had never seen mustard before, but he didn't want to admit such ignorance of fancy food to his cousin. So pretending that mustard was his favorite flavor of jam, he plunged his face into the jar and took a big mouthful. There was a moment of shock followed by a terrible burning that brought tears to his eyes. His mouth felt as if it were on fire!

Poor Abner ran about looking for something to put out the fire in his mouth. When he saw a glass of a pale, bubbly liquid, he climbed up to its rim and swigged it gratefully.

"Say!" he thought, when his mouth had finally cooled off, "this stuff tastes pretty good!" And before Monte could stop

him, Abner had drained the whole glass of champagne, bubbles and all.

Now a strange thing happened. Abner suddenly had a terrible attack of hiccups. And they were noisy. Every time the country mouse went "Hic!" his cousin would jump in alarm

and whisper, "Shush!" Whatever could have happened?
Abner wandered off to the other side of the table hoping the
little walk would clear his head. But to his dismay, he walked
smack into another mouse in a fancy green gelatin dessert.
They glared at each other, and then everything that Abner did

the gelatin mouse imitated in a most annoying fashion. Abner
was about to fight him when Monte pulled him away and said it
was time to get back to his mousehole.

Sorry to miss the chance of a good fight, Abner followed
Monte down to the floor where they hid beneath a chair.
There, not ten paces away, lay a big black cat, asleep, with its
back to them. "Oh boy!" thought Abner. "Now I'll get my
fight." And he started off toward the cat. But Monte pulled
him back sharply.

"Are you out of your mind?" he whispered. "That's
the cat!"

Abner shook him off and strode bravely up to the cat's

furry black backside. He gave it one swift kick, but his horrified cousin did not wait to see what would happen. He streaked for the safety of his mousehole and banged the door shut after him.

So there stood Abner quite alone, when the cat, enraged

at being awakened, turned with teeth bared and snarled at the mouse. All desire for a fight left Abner when he saw that fierce open mouth. He nearly jumped out of his little britches in fright.

Away he scampered with the cat in angry pursuit. The mousehole was shut tight, there was no place to hide, and Abner could feel the cat's breath on the back of his neck. And then, blessedly, he caught sight of an open window. Up he leaped to the sill, and out he dove to the roof with the cat following.

Luckily Abner fell down a drainpipe and made his escape to the street below, leaving the cat snarling on the roof. But the country mouse had simply traded one danger for dozens. What did he know about dodging city traffic, a mouse who had only had to worry about slow-moving cows and chickens and an old farm dog?

The street was a nightmare of speeding cars and people's hurrying feet. To make matters worse, the angry sound of horns blasted at the little mouse from all directions. "The

117

splendors of city life, indeed!" thought Abner as he darted every which way to avoid being run over. Finally he hitched a ride on a passing trolley and came safely at last to the city limits.

"From now on it's the simple country life for me," he vowed as he headed for his own little cottage and the green fields of home. "It's better to eat a crust in peace than a banquet in fear and trembling."

The Wise Little Hen

There once was a wise little hen who lived in a cozy little hen house with her brood of yellow chicks. The chicks had a fine time scratching and pecking in the front yard looking for things to eat.

One day the wise little hen came out to the yard carrying a basket of corn. "It's time to plant the corn, children," she said. "But it's much too much work for me alone. Come along and we'll see if one of our neighbors will help."

The chicks followed their mother to Peter Pig's house. Peter was playing his accordion and dancing a merry jig in front of his house.

"Good morning, friend pig," said the wise little hen. "I wonder if you'd help a neighbor out. I have this basketful of corn to plant, and it's too much work for me alone. Will you help me plant my corn?"

"Oh no, I can't," Peter Pig exclaimed. "I feel too sick. I

124

have an awful stomachache." And he tried his hardest to look very sick—at least until the wise little hen and her chicks were out of sight.

"Well, that's too bad, children," said the wise little hen. "Let's walk down to the river and see if friend duck will help." So off they went to Donald Duck's barge.

Donald was dancing a happy hornpipe on the deck. "Friend duck," said the wise little hen. "I have this basketful of corn to plant, and it's too much work for me alone. Will you help me plant my corn?"

At that Donald Duck clutched his stomach and moaned, "Oh no, I can't. I'm far too sick." And he staggered off as though he were in great pain.

"Too bad," clucked the wise little hen. "I'll have to plant it myself."

"No you won't, mother!" the little chicks cheeped. "We'll help you!" And they did. They hoed the cornfield and

then they plowed it while the wise little hen planted each
kernel of corn in its own little hole. Then the chicks watered
the field, and they all went home to wait.

Some weeks later, lo and behold! There was a field of fine
tall corn that made the hen and her chicks dance with joy.

"Well, now," said the wise little hen. "It's going to be
quite a job harvesting all that corn, and I'll need help. Let's
see if our neighbors will give us a hand."

And off the chickens went to find Peter Pig and Donald
Duck. The two of them were having a jolly time playing and
dancing at the Idle Hour Club. They tipped their hats and said
a polite hello to the wise little hen and her family.

"Neighbors," said the hen. "My corn has grown tall and ripe, and it's more than I can do to harvest it alone. Will you help me harvest my corn?"

"Who, me?" cried Peter Pig, clutching his stomach.

"We've got the bellyache again," groaned Donald Duck, looking very sick.

"Too bad," said the hen. But this time she was wise to their game. "I shall have to harvest it myself."

"We'll help! We'll help!" cheeped all the little chicks, and they did.

After the corn was harvested, the wise little hen brought it into her kitchen and cooked up a great feast. She made a huge pot of corn soup; she baked dozens of delicious corn muffins and a fragrant batch of corn bread. She boiled fresh ears of corn to serve slathered with butter, and she heaped all that good food on the table. It smelled wonderful!

Then she went out and called to her neighbors Peter Pig and Donald Duck. The minute they saw the wise little hen

those two thought she wanted help again. They began to moan
and groan and act very sick.

"Too bad," clucked the wise little hen. "I wanted you to
help me eat my corn."

"Who, me?" said Peter Pig, getting well again very quickly.

"Oh boy, oh boy," quacked Donald Duck, making a remarkable recovery.

In no time flat the two neighbors dashed over to the wise little hen's house, healthy and hungry and eager to start the feast that smelled so delicious.

"Here's something that will be just right for you," said the wise little hen giving them a big bowl, covered with a napkin, and two tablespoons to eat with. Donald and Peter drooled at the thought of the goodies that lay under the napkin. They were all set to dig in.

Peter Pig whisked the cover off the bowl, but—horrors! What was that staring up at him? A large bottle of castor oil!

133

Peter Pig didn't want it. Donald Duck didn't want it either.

What they both wanted was a share of the wonderful feast that the wise little hen and her chicks were enjoying inside the house.

Donald Duck and Peter Pig kicked each other all the way home.

Animal
Stories

Elmer

Elephant

ne fine day all the animal children in the forest were invited to Tillie Tiger's birthday party—the lion, the rhinoceros, the hippopotamus, the monkey, the fox, the raccoon, the chipmunk, and even Elmer Elephant.

Elmer was a very pleasant little elephant, and Tillie liked him a lot. But the other animals teased him and made fun of him because of his trunk. He was the only creature in the forest with such a long, curly nose, and the others used to laugh and laugh when they saw it. Naturally, that made Elmer sad when it happened. But otherwise he was a very happy young elephant.

So on this birthday away went Elmer through the forest, skipping and whistling a little tune and picking a bouquet of flowers for Tillie. When he came to Tillie's gate, he stopped and peeked shyly over it at the party.

All the animal children were gathered around the table in the yard singing to Tillie. And in the middle of the table was the most beautiful birthday cake Elmer had ever seen. It had delicious pink and white frosting in garlands and wreaths surrounding six lighted candles.

"Hello, Elmer!" Tillie called. "Come on in. You're just in time to watch me blow out my birthday candles."

Then Tillie saw the flowers Elmer was carrying. "Oh, Elmer, are those flowers for me?" she asked. "How sweet of you!" Elmer had never felt so happy.

Tillie looked at her cake with its candle flames dancing brightly. She made a silent wish, took a deep breath, and blew at the candles as hard as she could. The flames flattened out, then sprang up again. They did not go out. Once more Tillie took a deep, deep breath and blew as hard as she could. Once more the candles flickered—but they didn't go out. Then Tillie squeezed her little paws tightly closed, shut her eyes, and BLEW until her face turned red. The flames winked and blinked, then popped right back up again.

"Oh dear me," said Tillie Tiger. "Now what?"

"Let me try," offered the little hippo. He took a great huge breath, opened his big mouth wide, and blew up a storm.

139

"Swoosh!" The cake was blown right out from under its candles. Away it sailed on the hippo's breath, straight across the table, landing with a gooey plop right in Elmer Elephant's face.

Elmer was so surprised that he just stood there with pink and white frosting sliding down his cheeks and dripping down his curly trunk and his big floppy ears. The animal children laughed and laughed while poor Elmer stood there with his face growing pinker and pinker with embarrassment. It was terrible.

But Tillie Tiger didn't laugh at her friend. She wiped all the frosting off his face and kissed him right on the tip of his curly trunk. "That's all right, Elmer," she said. "Never mind. I'm going to go up and get us another cake."

But while Tillie went upstairs to her tree house, the other animals began to tease and make fun of Elmer. The monkey waved his hands near his head to look like Elmer's big flapping ears; the hippopotamus let a long flower stem hang

140

from the end of his nose, swinging it from side to side, to look like Elmer's trunk. The animal children danced around the little elephant laughing and screaming, "Funny Face Elmer! Big Nose Elmer! Ho, ho, Elmer! You take the cake!"

Elmer tried to smile bravely, but it just got worse and worse. The little hippo tweaked his trunk; the little monkey darted between his legs and tripped him. Down tumbled Elmer and over he rolled. Over and over he went, bouncing down the hill, spinning through the gate until he rolled PLUNK! smack up against a coconut tree. The coconuts dropped down, and some of them fell on Elmer. That hurt!

The little elephant sadly picked himself up and headed toward the forest. He felt terrible. When he came to a pond, he looked at his reflection in the water. It was true, he did have an awfully long trunk. Elmer tried to roll it up into a ball, but it unrolled. He tried to tuck it inside his shirt, but it wouldn't stay tucked. He even tried to tie his trunk into a knot, but it came undone and hung down as long as ever.

141

Two big tears trickled down Elmer's cheeks. It was hopeless.

Just then he heard a voice far above him. "Are you having nose trouble?" it asked. Elmer wiped his eyes and looked way, way up into the treetops. Old Mr. Giraffe was smiling down at him through the leaves.

"How did you know?" Elmer asked.

"Just figured, Elmer, just figured," said Mr. Giraffe kindly. "Used to have the same problem with my long neck. Lord, how I got teased and laughed at! Till they saw how I could eat all the tender top leaves no one else could reach. Then they stopped laughing. Same thing with noses."

Elmer sniffed and brushed away his tears.

"You want to see some funny-looking beaks," Mr. Giraffe continued, "just watch those pelicans over there with those big bags under their beaks. Those fellas are too busy eating all the good fish they can scoop up in their beaks to worry about being laughed at. Same with your trunk. You'll find plenty of use for it, don't worry."

Just then there was the noisy clang-clang-clang of a fire engine, and the pelicans flew up into the air cawing loudly. Above the treetops Mr. Giraffe could see smoke. "Looks like a fire!" he called down to Elmer. "Jump on and we'll have a look!"

Mr. Giraffe loped up the hill with Elmer hanging onto his long neck.

"It's Tillie Tiger's tree house," cried Elmer when they came close to the fire. "And she's up there on top of that high pole with fire all around her!"

"Don't worry, son," said Mr. Giraffe. "We'll save Tillie all right."

The other animal children were scurrying around on the ground every which way. They held out a blanket for Tillie to jump down into, but a piece of blazing wood dropped onto it, and the blanket went up in flames. The monkey children tried to climb the pole, but tongues of flame licked at them and drove them back down.

The firemen put up their hook and ladder, but the flames simply curled around it and burned it to the ground. It seemed as if nothing helped.

But then Mr. Giraffe and Elmer had a plan. Elmer climbed up on Mr. Giraffe's head. "Come on, boys!" the giraffe called to the pelicans. "Get your hose ready, Elmer!"

One by one the pelicans flew over to Elmer with their beaks full of water from the pond. Elmer sucked the water up into his trunk, aimed it at the fire, and WHOOSH! he sprayed a stream of water on the flames. Again and again he filled his trunk from the pelicans' beaks and sprayed until the fire sizzled and went out.

Then Elmer called to Tillie, "Don't be afraid, I'll save you!" And he wrapped his trunk snugly around her waist. Very gently Mr. Giraffe lowered his long neck so that Elmer and Tillie could step to the ground.

"My hero," cried Tillie Tiger, giving Elmer a big kiss.

All the animal children jumped with joy and gave a great loud cheer for Elmer Elephant, the hero with the wonderful trunk. But Elmer just folded one big ear over his face shyly. I wouldn't be surprised if he were smiling happily behind it!

Peculiar Penguins

Down under near the South Pole there lives an odd little bird called the penguin. Though he's a bird, he can swim—even under water—but even though he's a bird, he cannot fly. He has a funny walk—toes out, he waddles about in the icy world of the South Pole that is his home.

One day one of these peculiar penguins named Peter decided to go calling on Polly Penguin. He slicked himself up in front of an iceberg mirror, and off he toddled.

On the way, he passed a hole in the ice, and there in the water a school of delicious-looking puffer fish were jumping about.

"Just the thing for a gift to bring to Polly," thought Peter. And he dived into the water and caught a nice plump one.

Peter carried the puffer fish to Polly Penguin, who thanked him kindly and ate it in one big gulp. Peter was pleased that she liked his gift so much. But then something terrible happened.

The puffer fish puffed up inside of Polly. It blew up like a big balloon; and the worst of it was that poor Polly blew up with it till she looked as though she were ready to burst.

"What to do, what to do?" wondered Peter frantically as Polly squawked in distress.

Finally Peter had an idea. Standing behind Polly, he gave her a sudden hard kick. Sure enough, the puffer fish was knocked right out of Polly and leaped from her mouth back into the water.

Polly was her slim self again, but she was furious at Peter. "I'll never speak to you again, Peter Penguin," she said, and she slapped him and walked away in a huff. Then she climbed aboard a little ice floe and paddled out to sea.

Peter stood looking after her sadly. He had certainly messed things up with the girl he loved. But as he watched Polly sail farther and farther from shore, he was horrified to see a huge shark following her.

"Polly! Polly!" he yelled as loudly as he could. "Look out

behind you!" But Polly was still angry and refused to pay any attention to Peter's shouts.

There was just one thing for a brave penguin in love to do, and Peter did it. He grabbed a large stick, dived into the water, and swam lickety-split out to the shark. And he was just in the nick of time, for the ferocious creature had reared up and was about ready to snap at Polly with his sharp jagged teeth.

WHACK! Peter fetched the shark a terrible wallop with the stick right on his sensitive nose. Now the shark, furious at Peter, forgot about his dainty morsel and set out after her rescuer.

Off through the water they sped, Peter carrying the stick

in his mouth, the angry shark not far behind. Opening his jaws wide, the shark swallowed a school of little fish.

While his jaws were open, Peter turned and jammed his stick into the shark's mouth so it couldn't close again. Then he rescued the little fish, and all swam safely out and away, the fish leading Peter who waved tauntingly over his shoulder at his pursuer.

Unfortunately, he didn't see that the fish were heading for their favorite hiding place, a hole in the cliff that rose out of the sea. Into the hole the fish disappeared, but Peter Penguin, who was too large, slammed into the cliff.

And there was the shark right behind him, having managed to work the stick out of its mouth.

Peter clung to a small root on the side of the cliff and

153

looked down into the shark's toothy mouth. "Now I'm done for," he thought, trembling. But his trembling shook the root, and the root in turn shook a huge boulder that was delicately balanced overhead.

Just as the shark lunged for Peter, the boulder toppled into its open mouth—PLUNK! The heavy rock anchored the shark to the bottom of the sea, where the little fish gathered to see their enemy quite unable to harm them anymore.

And Peter? He and Polly Penguin got together, happy at last. They cuddled up close to each other, so close that from a distance the two penguins looked like a giant heart silhouetted against the brilliant southern lights.

154

Three Orphan Kittens

One blustery winter night when the wind howled and the snow blew this way and that, three little kittens were put out in the storm. Nobody wanted them; they were thrown over a garden wall in a bag and left to make their own way in the world.

The kittens were scared, and they were cold—almost ready to lie down in the snow and give up. But after they had managed to crawl out of the bag, the black kitten said, "Look. There's a house. And a window is banging. Maybe it's open a little crack, and we can get inside where it's warm."

The other kittens followed their brother, and sure enough, they managed to squeeze through a cellar window and found themselves in a dark basement. Luckily, cats—and even kittens—can see in the dark, and these three saw some stairs and climbed them. At the top of the stairs there was a door, and when the kittens pushed it ever so slightly with their little pink noses, it opened.

There before them was a large kitchen with a floor so shiny the kittens were startled to see their own faces looking up from it. But the exciting thing about that kitchen was its smells! The kittens took a big sniff.

158

"Someone is cooking cherries," said the gray kitten.

"And butter and sugar," said her ginger-colored sister whose mouth had begun to water.

Then they saw two big hands open the oven door and take out a scrumptious pie. They saw the pie placed on a table. And then two big feet walked out of the kitchen. Before you could say one-two-three, the three little kittens had scrambled up to the top of the table and made a delicious mess of the cherry pie.

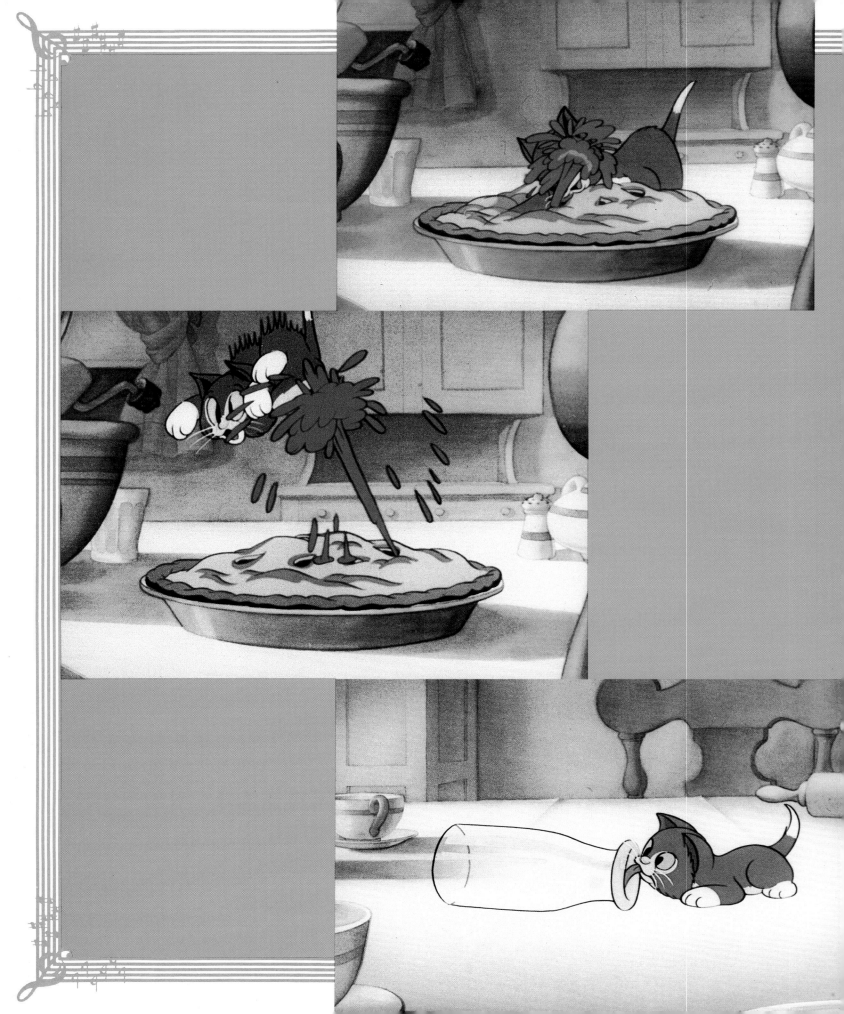

Next the kittens found a milk bottle and overturned it. The ginger kitten was licking the neck of the bottle when she greedily stuck her head too far into the opening and got stuck. Meanwhile her sister discovered a pepper shaker. When she slapped it, specks of pepper filled the air, making the three kittens sneeze and sneeze and sneeze. The ginger kitten finally sneezed her head right out of the milk bottle, but when she did, she fell to the floor pulling the tablecloth, silverware, dishes and all with a terrible crash down to the floor with her.

The frightened kittens streaked out of the kitchen and ran until they came to the nursery. While the black kitten found a big round ball that rolled away whenever he touched it, his sisters discovered a wonderful yellow-haired doll. When they pushed her she cried "Ma-ma!" That was such fun that the kittens took turns pushing the doll and listening to her say "Ma-ma!" until finally one of them pushed too hard, and the doll fell down and broke. Her pretty yellow wig came off and landed on top of the kitten's head, surprising her and her sister. Who had ever seen a kitten before with bright yellow curls?

Meanwhile the black kitten had found something remark-able in another room. It was a piano, and when he jumped onto its black-and-white keyboard from a nearby table, it made the most beautiful sounds. Every time he put a little paw down on a key, a different note sounded. But when he slapped at one

of the keys too hard, he accidentally pushed a button that made the piano play automatically. Then a roll of paper wound round and round, and the black-and-white keys moved up and down, playing a jouncy melody called "Kitten on the Keys."

Suddenly the piano roll came to an end, its paper flapped loudly, and the three kittens were so startled at the noise that they leaped from the keyboard to a nearby library table. But the black kitten didn't quite make it. His sharp little claws caught in the table cover, and with a terrifying crash down went a vase of flowers, a lamp, some books—and three horrified kittens.

There they cowered, trembling with fright amidst all the wreckage. They heard the sounds of heavy footsteps. They heard an angry voice. They felt big hands lift them by the scruff of the neck.

"Don't want any cats around here," boomed the voice. "Out you go!"

The front door was opened, and the kittens were about to be thrown out into the stormy night once again. They felt the cold wind and snowflakes blowing against their fur, and they shivered—when suddenly they heard a little girl's voice and saw little hands and arms reaching for them.

"Oh! Kittens! Aren't they cute? May I have them? Please! Oh, thank you!"

And the next thing they knew those three lucky kittens were tucked snug and warm into a doll's cradle. The little girl's hands were giving them doll bottles filled with warm milk, and the little girl's voice was crooning a sweet lullaby. The three orphan kittens had found a home.

Nature Stories

Flowers

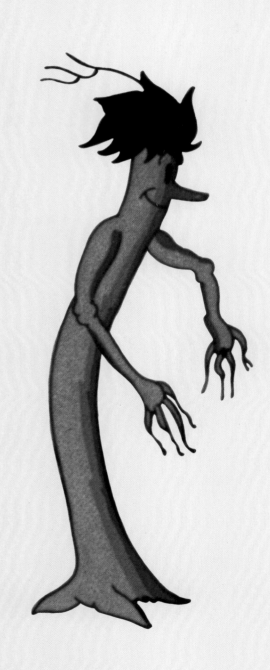

and Trees

ne morning at dawn the trees were still and deep in sleep when a bird flew to a branch on one of them and started to sing its little heart out. As the sky grew pinker and brighter, the bird warbled and chirped and tweeted a beautiful song praising the day and urging one and all to get up and enjoy it.

The trees awoke and stretched their limbs. The lilies awoke, the mushrooms awoke, the daisies opened their big black eyes and yawned. Then they washed by dipping their heads in the pool and shaking them in the water.

Suddenly everyone and everything was wide awake and very busy. The flowers and the mushrooms bent and swayed, performing their morning exercises. A slender young elm stooped beside the clear water where she could see her reflection and powdered her nose with a dandelion puff. She was lovely, and a young sapling who watched her longingly wished he dared speak to her.

But someone else was watching the elm, and he wanted her for his own. A hideous old tree, which had been blasted by lightning many years before and had burned in a forest fire, wanted the beautiful green-leaved elm to brighten his dreary corner of the woods. There all the trees were gnarled and leafless. Snakes and vipers lived in their hollow trunks, vultures perched on their crooked branches, and the remains of carrion strewed the ground. No flowers, no other things of beauty graced that haunted place. The old tree had decided

that he must take the graceful, leafy elm to live next to him.

Biding his time, he grabbed at her when she had finished her toilette. His spiky hands clutched her trunk, and he was about to carry her off when the young sapling came to the rescue.

They fought a duel with wooden clubs, and the sapling managed to free the elm and place her behind him while he

and the old tree battled it out. The sapling forced the old tree back step by step, and it was clear that the horrid old fellow was no match for the vigorous young sapling. But he had not lived so long without learning a few tricks of survival.

In a last desperate attempt to win the fight—and the beautiful elm—the old tree picked up the one weapon that forest-folk fear most horribly: FIRE!

Brandishing a burning torch, the wicked old tree leered at the elm and her protector. Then he threw it at their feet with all his might. Immediately small flames crackled through the underbrush and licked at the dry grasses. The elm shrank back terrified, while her brave sapling tried to stamp out the fire.

All the forest tried to help. The bluebells rang a shrill warning. The owl flew from tree to tree giving the alarm. Big trees tried to rescue small ones, the caterpillar disappeared underground, and some of the flowers near the edge of the pond formed a fire brigade, filling their cups with water and spraying it on the approaching flames.

At last some brave little birds with sharp beaks flew straight up in the sky where a small cloud floated. Then they lined up in a V-formation and dive-bombed the cloud. As their beaks punctured it, rain poured from the cloud. The flames hissed and died where the water hit them until only one small fire remained near the edge of the pool. And that was put out by the flower brigade.

The wicked old tree perished in his own fire, but everyone else was safe and rejoiced. The sapling serenaded his lady love on a harp strung on a nearby tree. At last he had the courage to tell her of his love in song while a chain of daisies formed themselves into a heart to make the message even clearer.

Dropping to one knee, the sapling proposed to the elm. To his delight she accepted, upon which the caterpillar emerged from the ground and rolled himself up to make a beautiful engagement ring.

And so the sapling and his lovely elm stood side by side,
their leafy branches intertwined. The bluebells rang out, the
birds sang, the daisies danced, and every living thing in the
forest rejoiced in their happiness.

The Old Mill

"What a fine place to build a nest!" exclaimed Mother and Father Robin the first time they saw the old windmill. Its sails were torn, and it stood, rather lopsided, on a small hill. But inside it was cool and quiet and shadowy. A perfect place to spend the spring and summer.

"And we'll have lots of good neighbors," said Father Robin looking around at spiders busily spinning their webs, mice scurrying about their business, an owl dozing on a rafter, bats hanging upside down from the roof, and a pair of cooing turtledoves perched in the window.

The robins built their nest just in time for Mother Robin to lay five bright blue eggs in it. Every day while she sat on them to keep them warm, Father Robin flew out to hunt for a fat, tasty worm to bring home for her supper.

181

One beautiful spring evening the sun set, turning the sky a rosy pink. All the daytime creatures headed homeward. The cows ambled from the pasture to their barn; the ducks waddled from the pond to the barnyard; and Father Robin flew home to his nest in the old mill. He had a plump worm in his beak for Mother Robin.

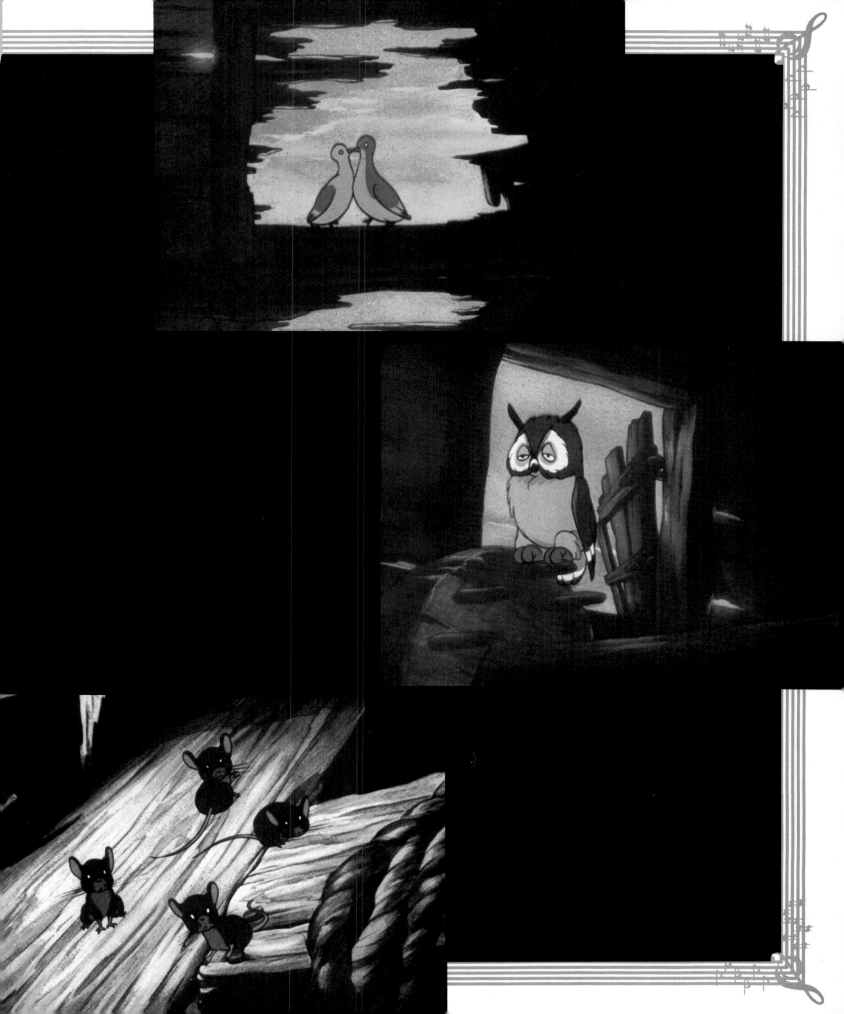

The two birds admired their pretty blue eggs. Carefully they turned them over. "Soon they will be ready to hatch," said Mother Robin. Then they both settled down for the night to keep the eggs warm. "Good night," they chirped sleepily to each other as they rubbed beaks.

Now it was the night creatures' turn to be up and doing. One by one the bats hanging from the rafters blinked their eyes open, unfolded their leathery wings, and yawned. With a whispery flapping of wings they streamed out of the mill and flew off into the twilight.

As the last rays of daylight faded from the sky, the pond grew dark, and the water lilies floating on it folded their petals tightly closed. The moon shone brightly in a black sky.

First one frog, then another, climbed out of the water onto a lily pad and began a chorus of croaking. The crickets in the

field chirped right along. The fireflies in the reeds around the pond blinked on and off. One flew too close to a hungry frog and WHOOSH! the frog snapped him up, and then the little lights continued to blink in his stomach.

Suddenly a wind blew up, tossing the reeds this way and that. The frogs dived off their lily pads and into the pond. A cloud swept across the moon. The sails of the old mill creaked as they began to turn in the wind. A loose shutter clattered and banged. The owl, disturbed from his nap, opened one big yellow eye and glared angrily.

As the sails of the mill turned now this way now that in the gusts of wind, the wooden cog wheel that was attached to them moved, coming closer and closer to the robins' nest, then retreating. The wheel strained and creaked against the rope that held it.

"Oh! Whatever shall we do?" cried Mrs. Robin, who had been awakened by the noise. A flash of lightning showed how close to the little nest the cogs were coming with every gust of wind.

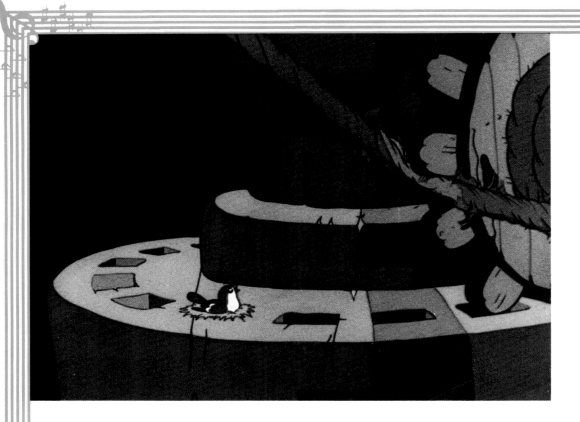

The old mill shuddered and shook, and now there was a
tremendous crash of thunder and a flare of lightning followed by
a sudden downpour of rain. Father Robin flew desperately in
and out of the cogs, looking for a way to stop the wheel. Mother
Robin huddled down over her precious eggs, determined to
protect them.

The shutters banged in the wind, the mice cowered together in a corner, the owl flew up to a higher rafter, where he
glared down crossly at the others every time a splash of water
bounced off his head. Only the turtledoves in the window
continued to murmur affectionately to each other and paid no
attention to the storm.

The rain came down harder and harder, and the angry wind
blew sheets of water into the old mill. The building shook and
shuddered, and the mill wheel creaked as it turned closer and
closer to the little nest. "I'm afraid we'll have to fly out of the
way soon," Father Robin said, "or the wheel will crush us."

"Never!" said Mother Robin bravely, spreading her wings
over her five blue treasures. "We must stay here and guard our
eggs."

Just then a bolt of lightning struck the mill with a terrible crash. The mill tipped away from the wind and settled with a groan deeper into its foundation. Suddenly the wind stopped, the great sails creaked to a standstill, and the mill wheel ground to a halt just inches from the nest!

It was very, very still and calm then, with only the faint rumble of the storm moving away in the distance. All the creatures in the mill settled down to sleep once more, and Mother Robin snuggled gratefully against Father Robin.

In the morning, the world outside was fresh and green. The cows ambled slowly back to their pasture, the ducks quacked happily on their way to the pond, while inside the mill something wonderful was happening in the robins' nest. The five blue eggs had cracked open, and five baby birds were cheeping hungrily, their little red mouths open as wide as could be.

"Keep an eye on our babies for us," the robins asked their neighbors. "With five hungry mouths to feed, we'll *both* have to go searching for worms."

As they flew out into the sunny morning, the robins looked back fondly at the old mill. "It's a lovely home for bringing up a family," they sang happily.

Water Babies

There is a magical world of fairy creatures on the
quiet lagoon, hidden from most human eyes. When
we see the lagoon just before sunrise, the water
lilies are tightly closed against the night, and birds are still
asleep in the branches of trees. But only a special few of us
have seen what happens when the first rays of the morning
sun warm the lily buds and their petals unfold and slowly
open.

There, nestled inside each flower, is a water baby sound
asleep. As the sun grows warmer and brighter, the babies
awaken and stretch. The tiny creatures frolic in the clear blue
water, splashing under a waterfall, ducking one another,
doing tricks, and playing games.

Sometimes there is a water parade with fantastic floats.
The water babies announce the start on flower trumpets while
riding the back of a big green turtle. A swan boat follows, and a
caterpillar gondola. There are butterfly sailboats and dragon-

flies gliding just above the water's surface towing delicate leaf canoes.

Sometimes there are sports contests with water babies racing on the backs of silvery fish to see who can streak across the lagoon fastest. In the bulrushes near the water's edge, they stage exciting rodeos. Cowboy water babies wearing Stetson hats made from flower blossoms ride bucking frogs. "Ride 'em cowbaby! Yippee!"

And the bravest red-headed toreador baby picks a bright red flower petal to use as a cape when he fights a bullfrog.

"Ai! Toro!" he calls as the gate to the bullfrog's pen is opened. Out rushes the fierce bullfrog. Twice the toreador waves the red petal in front of the enraged bullfrog. Twice he dodges the charge. The bullfrog finally charges into a flower that covers his head.

Not being able to see, the bullfrog slams his head into his pen, sits down hard, and to the cheers of the crowd tips the flattened hat to them. Gathered on blades of grass and leaves, the crowd of babies and insects decides that the toreador and the bullfrog have *both* won that fight!

This unseen world of the lagoon is filled with fun and frolic all the day long. Water babies bounce and frisk in the flower playground with their friends the turtles, caterpillars, birds, and insects.

But when the shadows begin to lengthen and the afternoon grows late, a small bug rings the evening bells. Then all the water babies know it is time to return to their water-lily beds. Some sail back in tiny leaf boats. Some are flown back in a bird's nest or on the backs of birds or dragonflies.

199

It has been a long and busy day. Tired water babies say their prayers. Then each curls up cozily in his lily bed and goes to sleep. As the sun sets and darkness falls, the water lilies fold closed to cover and protect the babies. Fireflies twinkle in the darkness.

Another day has ended on the quiet lagoon.

Poems
and
Rhymes

Old King Cole

The kingdom of Old King Cole is a magical book where nursery rhymes come to life on every page. Let's cross the drawbridge into this enchanted land and meet King Cole and his famous subjects, starting with the jolly monarch himself.

Old King Cole
Was a merry old soul,
And a merry old soul was he;
He called for his pipe,
And he called for his bowl,
And he called for his fiddlers three.

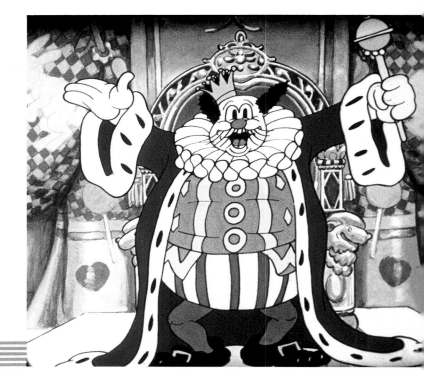

Little Boy Blue,
　　Come blow your horn,
The sheep's in the meadow,
　　The cow's in the corn.
What! Is this the way
　　You mind your sheep,
Under the haycock
　　Fast asleep?

There was a crooked man,
And he went a crooked mile,
He found a crooked sixpence
Against a crooked stile;
He bought a crooked cat
Which caught a crooked mouse,
And they all lived together
In a little crooked house.

Old Mother Hubbard
Went to the cupboard
　　To get her poor dog a bone;
But when she came there
The cupboard was bare,
　　And so the poor dog had none.

There was an old woman
    Who lived in a shoe,
She had so many children
    She didn't know what to do.
She gave them some broth
    Without any bread,
She whipped them all soundly
    And put them to bed.

All of these nursery rhyme characters have been invited to a ball in King Cole's castle, and so they troop over the drawbridge to be welcomed by the merry old soul. He is doing a lively war dance with the Ten Little Indians, but he welcomes them all heartily between steps.

Then some of the other guests take turns entertaining, with contrary Mistress Mary insisting on being first.

Mistress Mary,
Quite contrary,
How does your garden grow?
With silver bells
And cockle shells,
And pretty maids all in a row.

Peter, Peter, pumpkin eater,
Had a wife and couldn't keep her;
He put her in a pumpkin shell,
And there he kept her very well.

Jack Sprat could eat no fat,
His wife could eat no lean;
So between the two of them
They licked the platter clean.

Three blind mice!
  See how they run!
They all ran after the farmer's wife,
Who cut off their tails with a carving knife.
Did you ever see such a thing in your life
  As three blind mice?

And now the hour is growing late, and it is time for the party to be over. Though the clock says midnight, it chimes just once.

Hickory, dickory, dock,
  The mice ran up the clock;
  The clock struck one,
    The mice ran down,
      Hickory, dickory, dock.

Old King Cole, laughing and chuckling, shakes hands with all his guests and wishes them a good night. He is especially glad to see that Little Bo-peep has found her sheep at last, and he tosses her into the air until she giggles with delight.

One by one they all return to their homes. King Cole leaves his empty milk bottle out for the milkman and takes himself off to bed.

Finally everyone is asleep and dreaming sweet dreams while the man in the moon smiles down on the happy kingdom and keeps watch over it all the night long.

Little

Hiawatha

By the shores of Gitchee Gumee, near the shining Big-Sea-Water, little Hiawatha lived with his Indian tribe. He wished most of all to become an Indian brave like his father, a great hunter, a fearless warrior, one who knew all the secrets of the river and the forest.

One day Hiawatha took his canoe of birch bark and paddled down the river and through the canyon. He heard the lapping of the waters and the sounds of music from the pine trees. "Minne-wawa!" said the pine trees. "Mudway-aushka!" said the waters.

Little Hiawatha came to a great waterfall, but he paddled his canoe behind the waterfall and out again without a drop of water falling on him. Through a whirlpool in the river, which whirled the birch canoe in circles, little Hiawatha bravely paddled on.

For he'd come to hunt the red deer, hunt the rabbit, hunt

the squirrel, and the great bear. Fearless was this mighty warrior and skilled in all the craft of hunters!

Hiawatha stopped his canoe near the bank of the river. As he got out, he stood with one moccasined foot on the bank and the other on the edge of the canoe, as he had seen his father do. He held his hand to his eyes and looked around, as he had seen the braves do. But what was wrong?

The canoe slipped out into the stream, and Hiawatha landed with a splash in the water! From the forest came the sounds of animals laughing. Angrily, Hiawatha climbed up onto the river bank and stalked into the forest, his little bow and arrow in his hands. He would show them he was a hunter not to be laughed at!

He chased three squirrels through the forest, but they scampered up a tree and escaped. He discovered strange animal tracks on the ground and heard a strange stomping sound. What dangerous creature could this be?

Following the tracks and the sound, brave Hiawatha found himself face to face with a—grasshopper. He aimed his bow and arrow, but just at that moment his deerskin pants fell down. As Hiawatha paused to pull up his pants, the grasshop-

215

per leaped away, and once again there was the sound of
animals laughing in the forest.

Angrily, Hiawatha chased a group of rabbits through the
forest. They all got away except one baby rabbit who hopped
up on a tree stump and was cornered by the fearless hunter.
Hiawatha yelled "Yippee!" and did the terrifying war dance
of the Indian braves. Then he prepared to shoot the rabbit.
Trembling with fright, the baby rabbit waited for Hiawatha's
arrow to finish him off. But just as Hiawatha drew back on
his bow, his pants fell down again.

As he pulled them back up, he was eye to eye with the
rabbit, and he saw a large tear roll down the little fellow's face.
Hiawatha felt so sorry that he lowered his bow and arrow and
let the rabbit run in safety to join his family. The mighty
hunter did not have the heart to shoot such a helpless little
creature.

Hiawatha picked up his bow and arrow and looked at them angrily. They were of no use to an Indian brave who could not bear to harm any of the animals. He broke them over his knee and threw the pieces away. At that, loud cheers and shouts went up from all the forest creatures who were hiding behind trees and watching Hiawatha's every move with bright eyes. They jumped up and down with joy and applauded him.

Embarrassed, Hiawatha backed away from the grateful animals and ran off deeper into the forest where he could still hear their cheers faintly. He sighed sadly. He would never be a hunter, but maybe he could be a great tracker, following animals and learning all about them.

Just then Hiawatha noticed some large paw prints on the ground. He got down on his hands and knees to examine them. He put his ear to the ground as he had seen the braves do, to listen for an animal's footsteps. And he crawled along the ground on all fours, following the big tracks.

Meanwhile, a small bear cub came out of his cave, sniffing along the ground. Suddenly, BUMP! The cub and Hiawatha knocked heads. They looked up, face to face, each made a

frightened sound, and the cub ran away as fast as his little legs
could go. Hiawatha ran after him, only wanting to be friends.

The cub ran to a large brown rock, jumped on top of it,
and hid on the other side. Hiawatha followed, jumping on top
of the rock, too. But the rock was soft; it moved, and then it
growled so loudly that the forest echoed. It was no rock, but a
huge, fierce mother bear who had been taking a nap nearby.
She lumbered to her feet and tried to knock Hiawatha off her
back. He caught at the bear's nose as he fell and found
himself looking into a hideous mouth full of sharp bear teeth.
Roaring, the bear shook her head and tossed Hiawatha to the
ground; then she started after him.

And now all the forest animals were alerted that their new
friend was in danger. The beavers beat out a message with
their flat tails on a hollow log. Three raccoons scampered up a
tree, grabbed a long vine, and waited till Hiawatha ran past.
Then they stretched the vine across the path and tripped the
bear who was chasing him.

220

The beavers gnawed down a tree and made a log boat to ferry Hiawatha across the river. But the bear wasn't far behind him, and she made a great dive onto one end of the log. Up flew Hiawatha into the air. He grabbed onto a branch of a tree and continued climbing up, up, up, for all he was worth.

But the bear clambered out of the water, and she quickly started up the tree after Hiawatha. In no time the three beavers followed, and they went to work busily gnawing at the tree trunk. Just as the bear was about to grab Hiawatha at the very tiptop of the tree, the tree began to sway and fall with Hiawatha and the bear clinging to it for dear life. A family of opossums in the nearby trees caught Hiawatha in midair. Hanging by their tails from the branches, they passed the little Indian from one to another, swinging him through the air safely away from the bear who had fallen to the ground.

In the meantime, a little fawn had been harnessed to two branches that formed a carrier. The opossums deposited

Hiawatha neatly on the carrier, some friendly squirrels handed him the reins, and off went the fawn wagon speeding through the woods to the shore of the lake. There the forest creatures helped Hiawatha into his canoe and watched from the shore as their new friend turned his canoe homeward.

So it was that Hiawatha came to the end of his day of hunting. And the beaver called him brother, while the rabbit and the red squirrel and the little deer that watched him thought of him as a friend departing.

Mighty hunter Hiawatha!

Mighty chieftain Hiawatha!

Mighty little Hiawatha!

The Night Before Christmas

by Clement C. Moore

'Twas the night before Christmas,
when all through the house
Not a creature was stirring, not even a mouse;
The stockings were hung by the chimney with care,
In hopes that St. Nicholas soon would be there;
The children were nestled all snug in their beds,
While visions of sugar-plums danced in their heads;
And mamma in her 'kerchief, and I in my cap,
Had just settled our brains for a long winter's nap,
When out on the lawn there arose such a clatter,
I sprang from the bed to see what was the matter.
Away to the window I flew like a flash,
Tore open the shutters and threw up the sash.

The moon on the breast of the new-fallen snow
Gave the lustre of mid-day to objects below,
When, what to my wondering eyes should appear,
But a miniature sleigh, and eight tiny reindeer,

With a little old driver, so lively and quick,
I knew in a moment it must be St. Nick.
More rapid than eagles his coursers they came,
And he whistled, and shouted, and called them by name:
"Now, *Dasher!* now, *Dancer!* now, *Prancer* and *Vixen!*
On, *Comet!* on, *Cupid!* on, *Donder* and *Blitzen!*
To the top of the porch! to the top of the wall!
Now dash away! dash away! dash away all!"

As dry leaves that before the wild hurricane fly,
When they meet with an obstacle, mount to the sky,
So up to the house-top the coursers they flew,
With the sleigh full of toys, and St. Nicholas too.
And then, in a twinkling, I heard on the roof
The prancing and pawing of each little hoof.
As I drew in my head, and was turning around,
Down the chimney St. Nicholas came with a bound.

He was dressed all in fur, from his head to his foot,
And his clothes were all tarnished with ashes and soot;
A bundle of toys he had flung on his back,
And he looked like a peddler just opening his pack.

His eyes—how they twinkled! his dimples how merry!
His cheeks were like roses, his nose like a cherry!
His droll little mouth was drawn up like a bow,
And the beard of his chin was as white as the snow;
The stump of a pipe he held tight in his teeth,
And the smoke it encircled his head like a wreath;
He had a broad face and a little round belly,
That shook, when he laughed, like a bowlful of jelly.
He was chubby and plump, a right jolly old elf,
And I laughed when I saw him, in spite of myself;
A wink of his eye and a twist of his head,
Soon gave me to know I had nothing to dread;

He spoke not a word, but went straight to his work,
And filled all the stockings; then turned with a jerk,
And laying his finger aside of his nose,
And giving a nod, up the chimney he rose;

He sprang to his sleigh, to his team gave a whistle,
And away they all flew like the down of a thistle.
But I heard him exclaim, ere he drove out of sight,
"Happy Christmas to all, and to all a goodnight."

Wynken,

Blynken, and Nod

by Eugene Field

Wynken, Blynken, and Nod one night
    Sailed off in a wooden shoe,—
    Sailed on a river of crystal light
Into a sea of dew.
"Where are you going, and what do you wish?"
    The old moon asked the three.
"We have come to fish for the herring fish
    That live in this beautiful sea;
Nets of silver and gold have we!"
            Said Wynken,
            Blynken,
            And Nod.

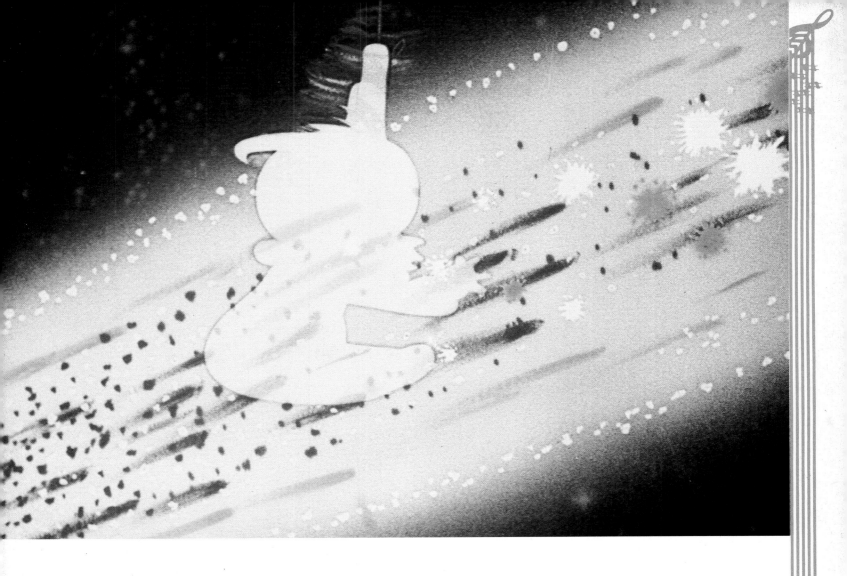

The old moon laughed and sang a song,
As they rocked in the wooden shoe;
And the wind that sped them all night long
Ruffled the waves of dew.
The little stars were the herring fish
That lived in that beautiful sea—
"Now cast your nets wherever you wish,—
Never afeard are we!"
So cried the stars to the fishermen three,
Wynken,
Blynken,
And Nod.

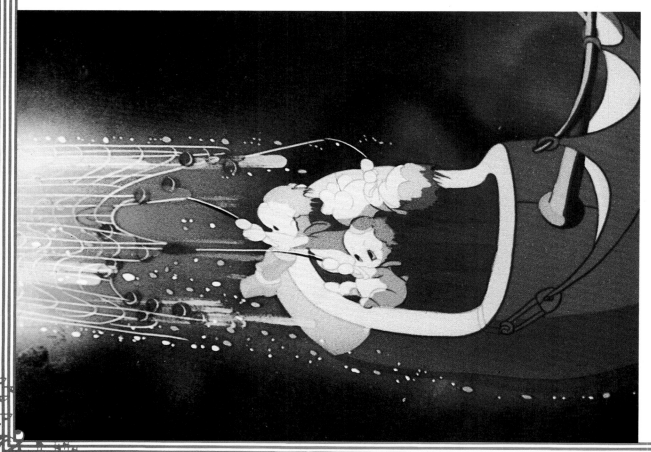

All night long their nets they threw
    To the stars in the twinkling foam,—
Then down from the skies came the wooden shoe,
    Bringing the fishermen home:
'Twas all so pretty a sail, it seemed
    As if it could not be;
And some folk thought 'twas a dream they'd dreamed
    Of sailing that beautiful sea;
But I shall name you the fishermen three:
        Wynken,
        Blynken,
        And Nod.

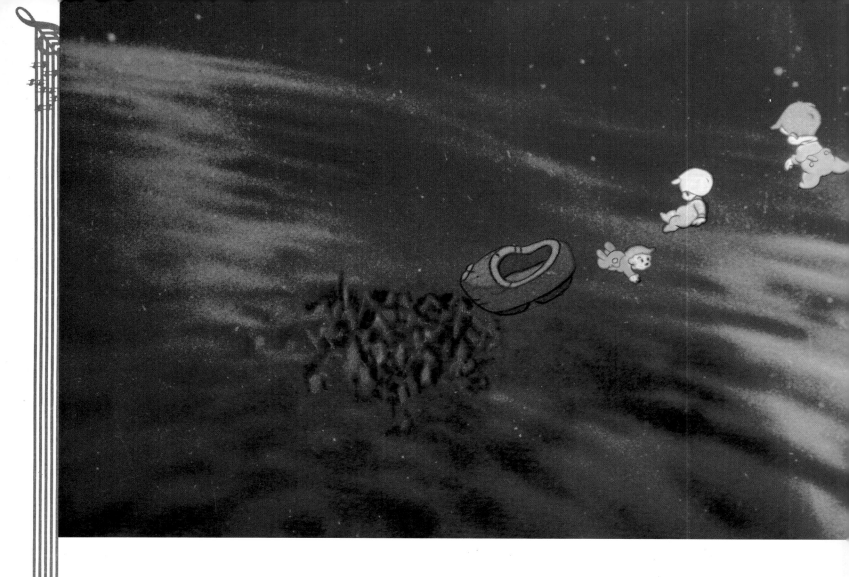

Wynken and Blynken are two little eyes,
    And Nod is a little head,
And the wooden shoe that sailed the skies
    Is a wee one's trundle-bed;
So shut your eyes while Mother sings
    Of wonderful sights that be,
And you shall see the beautiful things
    As you rock in the misty sea
Where the old shoe rocked the fishermen three:—
        Wynken,
        Blynken,
        And Nod.

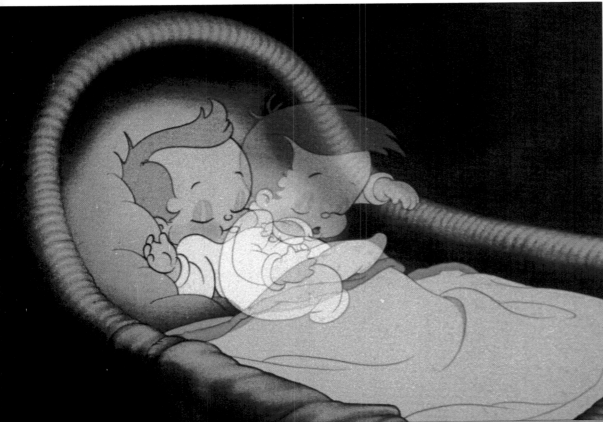

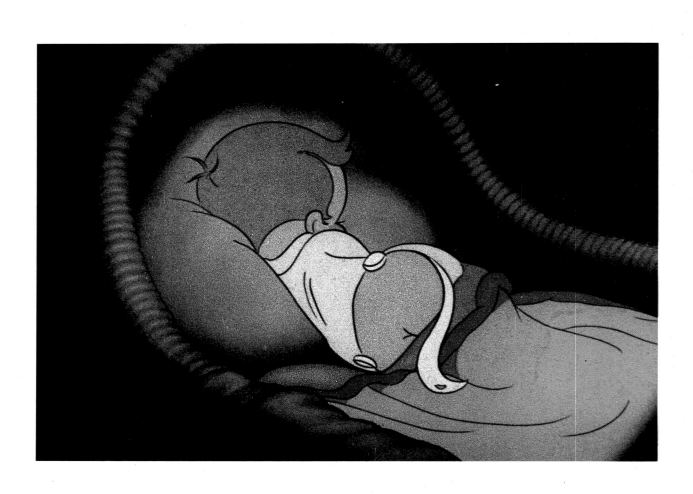

Filmography of Silly Symphonies

In the decade between 1929 and 1939 the Walt Disney Studio produced a series of seventy-six cartoon shorts combining music and animation. The first twenty-eight were in black and white; the balance were created in full color. Although the internationally famous Mickey Mouse, who starred in a dazzlingly successful series of his own, was credited with "presenting" each Silly Symphony, he did not appear in any of them.

The first animated short ever to be produced in color, *Flowers and Trees*, was a Silly Symphony, and the innovative brilliance exhibited in all these little films was to burgeon into the great full-length classics of the next three decades. Meanwhile, eight Academy Awards for Best Short Subject were garnered by Walt Disney's Silly Symphonies, many of which continue to delight young and old to this very day.

Title	Year
The Skeleton Dance	1929
El Terrible Toreador	1929
Springtime	1929

Title	Year
Hell's Bells	1929
The Merry Dwarfs	1929
Summer	1930
Autumn	1930
Cannibal Capers	1930
Night	1930
Frolicking Fish	1930
Arctic Antics	1930
Midnight in a Toy Shop	1930
Monkey Melodies	1930
Winter	1930
Playful Pan	1930
Birds of a Feather	1931
Mother Goose Melodies	1931
The China Plate	1931
The Busy Beavers	1931
The Cat's Out	1931
Egyptian Melodies	1931
The Clock Store	1931
The Spider and the Fly	1931
The Fox Hunt	1931
The Ugly Duckling	1931
The Bird Store	1932
The Bears and the Bees	1932
Just Dogs	1932

Title	Year
* Flowers and Trees	1932
King Neptune	1932
Bugs in Love	1932
Babes in the Woods	1932
Santa's Workshop	1932
Birds in the Spring	1933
Father Noah's Ark	1933
* Three Little Pigs	1933
Old King Cole	1933
Lullaby Land	1933
The Pied Piper	1933
The Night Before Christmas	1933
The China Shop	1934
The Grasshopper and the Ants	1934
Funny Little Bunnies	1934
The Big Bad Wolf	1934
The Wise Little Hen	1934
The Flying Mouse	1934
Peculiar Penguins	1934
The Goddess of Spring	1934
* The Tortoise and the Hare	1935
The Golden Touch	1935
The Robber Kitten	1935
Water Babies	1935
The Cookie Carnival	1935

Title	Year
Who Killed Cock Robin?	1935
Music Land	1935
* Three Orphan Kittens	1935
Cock o' the Walk	1935
Broken Toys	1935
Elmer Elephant	1936
Three Little Wolves	1936
Toby Tortoise Returns	1936
Three Blind Mouseketeers	1936
* The Country Cousin	1936
Mother Pluto	1936
More Kittens	1936
Woodland Cafe	1937
Little Hiawatha	1937
* The Old Mill	1937
The Moth and the Flame	1938
Wynken, Blynken, and Nod	1938
Farmyard Symphony	1938
Merbabies	1938
Mother Goose Goes Hollywood	1938
Ferdinand the Bull (originally planned as a Silly Symphony, but released instead as a special short)	1938
The Practical Pig	1939
* The Ugly Duckling (remake)	1939

* Academy Award for Best Short Subject